BOOKS BY

CHESTER G. STARR

THE ORIGINS OF GREEK CIVILIZATION:
1100–650 B.C. (1961)

THE AWAKENING OF THE GREEK
HISTORICAL SPIRIT (1968)

These are Borzoi Books, published in New York by
Alfred · A · Knopf

THE AWAKENING OF

THE GREEK HISTORICAL SPIRIT

THE

AWAKENING

OF THE GREEK

HISTORICAL SPIRIT

by Chester G. Starr

PROFESSOR OF HISTORY

UNIVERSITY OF ILLINOIS

ᒍᒍᒍᒍᒍᒍᒍᒍᒍᒍᒍᒍᒍᒍᒍᒍᒍᒍᒍᒍᒍ

New York · ALFRED A. KNOPF · 1968

THIS IS A BORZOI BOOK

PUBLISHED BY ALFRED A. KNOPF, INC.

First Edition

© Copyright 1968 by Chester G. Starr

Library of Congress Catalog Card Number: 68–12679

Manufactured in the United States of America

TO

NORRIS L. BROOKENS

SCHOLAR, DOCTOR, AND FRIEND

PREFACE

HISTORY is a way of assessing the human experience which has been much cultivated in recent generations. Once upon a time, however, history did not exist as a formal discipline, largely because men did not yet look at their past as a series of real events connected with the present. The awakening of such an attitude in early Greece, the historical spirit proper, is the subject of the present work.

Any explanation of this remarkable development must be set against the broad background of the archaic period of Greek civilization, an era difficult to study but absorbingly fresh, exuberant, in many ways naïve. History was not a derivative art, dependent on philosophy, tragedy, or any of the other great creations of Greek civilization as a source for its inner substance and methods of research; our search for its real roots may illuminate the enduringly fundamental qualities of the historical approach.

Since some readers of this book may be without Greek, I have provided translations of Greek passages. Wherever the Loeb Classical Library provides an adequate version, I have normally used it, except for Herodotus (George Rawlinson) and the philosophic fragments (Kathleen Freeman). Other translations are indicated in the relevant notes unless I have made my own renderings. On occasion, however, it is important to have the original Greek as well. The sources for the illustrations are given in the List of Plates.

To all who smoothed my path in three recent trips to Europe I am grateful; in particular the staff of the American School of Classical Studies in Athens has been most helpful on two of these occasions.

CHESTER G. STARR

Urbana, Illinois
March 8, 1967

CONTENTS

Introduction   3

Chapter 1: The World of Epic and Myth   12
Homer and History 13 . . . Legacy of Myth and Epic 23 . . . Contributions of the Near East 25 . . . The Later Eighth Century 32

Chapter 2: The Expansion of Greece   37
A Sense of Space 41 . . . Greeks and Barbarians 49

Chapter 3: The Framework of Time   57
Continuity and Conservatism 61 . . . The Awareness of Time 64 . . . Historical Time 69

Chapter 4: Man and the State   78
The Rise of Political Life 80 . . . The Audience of the Polis 85 . . . Human Self-Awareness 91

Chapter 5: The Intellectual Development of the Sixth Century   99
The Rise of Disciplined Thought 101 . . . The Road of Speculative Reason 107 . . . The Road of Factual Research 111 . . . The Archaic Age 117

Chapter 6: The Appearance of History   120
The Historical Spirit in Arts and Letters 121 . . . Herodotus, Father of History 132

Chapter 7: The Onward March of History   147

Bibliography   152

Index   follows page   157

ILLUSTRATIONS

FACING PAGE 78

I · The World of Homer
Prothesis scene from Dipylon amphora (National Museum 200, Athens). Photograph courtesy Alison Frantz.

II · The Sixth Century
(a) Dionysus in his ship, cup by Exekias (Antikensammlung 2044, Munich). Photograph courtesy the Museum.
(b) Youth from Sunium (National Museum 3344, Athens). Photograph courtesy Deutsches Archäologisches Institut, Athenische Abteilung.

III · The Arcesilaus Cup
Laconian cup (Cabinet des Médailles 4899 [2707], Paris). Photograph courtesy Hirmer Fotoarchiv, Munich.

IV · Croesus on His Pyre
Amphora by Myson (Musée du Louvre G 197, Paris). Photograph courtesy Hirmer Fotoarchiv, Munich.

V · Scythians and Persians
(a) Scythian archer, plate by Epictetus (British Museum E 135, London). Photograph courtesy Trustees of the British Museum.
(b) Persians, from Attic vase c. 450 (Staatliche Museen F 3156, Berlin). Photographs courtesy the Museum.

VI · *Death in the Fifth Century*

Loutrophoros by Kleophrades painter (National Museum 1170, Athens). Photograph courtesy Hirmer Fotoarchiv, Munich.

VII · *Narrative in the Sixth and Fifth Centuries*

(a) Battle of gods and giants, from the Siphnian frieze (Delphi Museum). Photograph courtesy Alison Frantz.

(b) Heracles and the priests of Busiris, pelike by Pan painter (National Museum 9683, Athens). Photograph courtesy Deutsches Archäologisches Institut, Athenische Abteilung.

VIII · *The Mourning Athena*

Relief from Acropolis (Acropolis Museum 695, Athens). Photograph courtesy Alison Frantz.

Chronological Table page 40

ABBREVIATIONS

CVA *Corpus Vasorum Antiquorum*

Fränkel, *DuP* Hermann Fränkel, *Dichtung und Philosophie des frühen Griechentums* (2d ed.; Munich, 1962).

FGrH Felix Jacoby, *Fragmente der griechischen Historiker* (Berlin-Leiden, 1923–).

Guthrie, *Greek Philosophy*, I, II W. K. C. Guthrie, *A History of Greek Philosophy*, I: *The Earlier Presocratics and the Pythagoreans* (Cambridge, 1962); II: *The Presocratic Tradition from Parmenides to Democritus* (Cambridge, 1965).

Herodot Herodot: Eine Auswahl aus der neueren Forschung, ed. Walter Marg (Munich, 1962).

Jaeger, *Paideia*, I Werner Jaeger, *Paideia: Die Formung des griechischen Menschen,* I (3d ed.; Berlin, 1954).

Peek Werner Peek, *Griechische Vers-Inschriften,* I: *Grab-Epigramme* (Berlin, 1955).

PW Pauly, Wissowa, et al., *Real-Encyclopädie der classischen Altertumswissenschaft* (Stuttgart, 1894–).

Starr, *Origins* Chester G. Starr, *The Origins of Greek Civilization, 1100–650 B.C.* (New York, 1961).

Tod, *GHI*, I Marcus N. Tod, *A Selection of Greek Historical Inscriptions,* I: *To the End of the Fifth Century B.C.* (2d ed.; Oxford, 1946).

Fragments of archaic poets are cited from the edition of Ernst Diehl, *Anthologia lyrica graeca* (2d–3d edd.; Leipzig, 1936–52); those of early philosophers, from H. Diels and W. Kranz, *Die Fragmente der Vorsokratiker* (3d ed.; Berlin, 1954); tragic fragments, from A. Nauck and B. Snell, *Tragicorum graecorum fragmenta* (Hildesheim, 1964).

THE AWAKENING OF

THE GREEK HISTORICAL SPIRIT

INTRODUCTION

MANY PEOPLES have had folk memories, but only three seem independently to have evolved the concept of formal written history. One of these is the Chinese; the second is the Hebrew; the third, and most significant for all later Western culture, is the Greek. The idea of explaining man's present condition by a disciplined, factual description of his past is one of the great achievements which we owe to Hellenic creativeness; neighboring cultures as well, from the rise of Islam on, have drawn their idea of history from Greek models.

My objective in the following pages is to explore the slow awakening of this historical spirit in the early centuries of Greek civilization, roughly 700–450 B.C. The work "awakening" I have deliberately chosen to suggest some important aspects of my interpretation of this process. Many of the factors required for a historical view were deep-rooted in the Hellenic world, but beside them were others which made it extremely difficult for the Greeks to create a consciously historical outlook. Both sides must be kept in mind, and in balance, if we are to understand why history, a sophisticated means by which man accounts to himself for his nature, arose late and gained incomplete dominance in Greek culture.

Also implicit in my use of the word "awakening" is a firm belief that history did not suddenly emerge as a simple reflex to Athenian pride in empire, the jubilation of the Greeks over their almost miraculous defeat of the Persian onslaught, or any other single characteristic of fifth-century society. The Father of History, Herodotus, did appear at this time, and the

3

manner in which he thought and wrote was undoubtedly affected by the currents of his age. Still, much of the past development of Hellas influenced him even more strongly; another aspect, not often considered despite its crucial importance, is the fact that Greek civilization had produced an audience equipped with historical attitudes and interests.

Without this audience the history of Herodotus either would never have been written or would have passed away without lasting effect. The chains of thought about space, time, and other factors which lay behind Herodotus and his auditors were long and complicated, and it is on their evolution that I propose to focus attention. Insofar as any consideration has been devoted to this subject, the picture of historical manifestations before Herodotus is usually a rather elementary one. First comes Homer, who tells a tale clearly laid in the past, even if of doubtfully historical events; then the epic cycle elaborates the Trojan story, and philosophers appear to add a dash of logic; about 500 B.C. Hecataeus travels over the world and also rationalizes early myth; and finally Herodotus transfers the scene of his particular tale to a real event, the Persian invasion of Greece. The "source and spring" of history is, in this view, simple wonder or curiosity.

Yet, as one wise student of historiography has observed, "There was no Herodotus before Herodotus."[1] We cannot, that is to say, simply use Hecataeus and his contemporaries as sufficient antecedent for Herodotus, nor will this method of approach disentangle the basic factors involved in the awakening of the historical spirit. Some of these lie implicit in the Homeric outlook, so one must properly begin with Homer and the other evidence for the earliest stage of Greek culture

[1] A. Momigliano, *Studies in Historiography* (New York: Harper Torchbook, 1966), p. 129; see also the thoughtful essay by Wolfgang Schadewaldt, "Die Anfänge der Geschichtschreibung bei den Griechen," *Die Antike*, X (1934), pp. 144–68. The principal source of the scheme sketched in the previous paragraph is perhaps Friedrich Creuzer, *Die historische Kunst der Griechen in ihrer Entstehung und Fortbildung* (1803).

4

before 700 B.C. Principally, however, my main concern will be the crucial era, the archaic period from 700 to 500; and in this I shall seek to disentangle, chapter by chapter, the strands which are particularly relevant—first, the development of a sense of space and the differentiation of peoples in this geographical framework; secondly, the growing awareness of time as a continuous dimension within which human changes occur; thirdly, the consolidation of the city-state and the companion self-awareness of its citizens; and fourthly, the crystallization of intellectual processes in poetry and art as well as in philosophy.

These elements were not independently conceived in the archaic era; nor are space, time, and man as rigorously distinct ingredients in modern historical writing as the present analysis must take them to be. But after their development has been isolated we can proceed to put them back together in the poetry of Pindar and the first real history, that of Herodotus.

Let me observe here that when Herodotus begins to write, my tale is done; there is no need to furnish once again a detailed commentary on his amazing genius. The following pages will not often go on beyond Herodotus to talk of his great successor Thucydides, a decision which rests primarily on the fact that Herodotus directly and admirably represents the culmination of the developments on which our attention will be focused. Not only by reason of Thucydides' own personality and interests but also because of the supervening sophistic movement the history of Thucydides is of a markedly different stamp, at least on the surface; for in more respects than is commonly admitted Thucydides built on the foundations laid by Herodotus.

My study must appear in a sense as an intellectual history of early Greece, but it is not my intent to describe this majestic evolution in all its particulars or to be drawn aside into the many thorny issues which invite divagation. Some aspects of special relevance we must look at very carefully; others can only be sketched in general terms, which would properly be

qualified in detail by specialists in philosophy, art, or literature. In any case I am skeptical of two major methods of
attack often favored nowadays: on the one hand the sweeping, dogmatic reconstruction which is based on no more than
a few facts, isolated from their original contexts by the ravages
of time; and on the other the extremely detailed manipulation
of a specific statement, the result of which is likely to be the
discovery of hidden meanings of very dubious validity.

The poets and philosophers of the era, one must always
remember, survive for the most part only in fragments; so too
its statues and vases often stand broken or incomplete in
modern museums. Yet enough remains for us to see at least the
main lines of evolution, though one must repeatedly regret the
lack of that mass of information which would enable us to
furnish firm, detailed connections and also to observe the
byways and dead ends attending any cultural pattern. Even so
we must wander into poetic and artistic paths which students
of historiography rarely traverse, for here lies the evidence on
contemporary views of space, time, and man.

Not only is the evidence scattered and unusual; the world
we are about to enter is very different from modern society.
To underline this fact, we may consider first a few words
which will recur repeatedly. One is "history" itself, which
comes from the Greek *historia*. This appears in Homer in a
cognate form meaning one who "sees" something and so is
judge or arbiter; thereafter *historia* has a variety of unspecial-
ized meanings in early Greek literature.[2] Chief among these
came to be that of "investigation" or "research"; Herodotus
thus begins his great work:

> These are the researches of Herodotus of Halicarnassus,
> which he publishes, in the hope of thereby preserving from de-
> cay the remembrance of what men have done, and of prevent-
> ing the great and wonderful actions of the Greeks and the

[2] Homer, *Iliad* 18.501, 23.486; note other examples in Liddell-Scott-
Jones, *Greek-English Lexicon s.v.* ἴστωρ; F. Muller, "De 'historiae'
vocabulo atque notione," *Mnemosyne*, LIV (1926), pp. 234–57.

Barbarians from losing their due meed of glory; and withal to put on record what were their grounds of feud.

Neither Herodotus nor his immediate successor, Thucydides, seems to have called his written work a History; Thucydides, indeed, gives the term *Syngraphe,* that which is written down or "narrative," as if it were a proper term for "history." [3] Common application of the word *historia* to the written product came only in the fourth century B.C.

Similar fluidity or lack of precision attends a great variety of concepts which one must use in assessing the rise of Greek historical writing. In the preface of Herodotus just quoted the word *aitia* is translated "grounds," and usually we take it as meaning "cause"; but whether Herodotus himself clearly saw in *aitia* a connection of cause and effect or simply a source of guilt is debatable. So too *nomos* means now "custom," now "law"; the term for the city-state, *polis,* is the root of our word "political," but Greek political organization and thought often must jar a modern citizen of a nation-state in their particular twists and unwritten assumptions. To analyze within the confines of the present work all the complexities and nuances of such terms would take us far afield; yet their nature must be kept in mind, and at least occasionally it will be better to leave a Greek word untranslated in a specific discussion.

The problems which modern students face in assessing Greek historical writing are not purely verbal, for in the Hellenic outlook there were fundamental characteristics which may easily mislead us. In general, students of historiography have the right, even the duty, to think of history in the light of all the clarification of its meaning which modern study has produced; but they must not then go on to demand that authors of earlier eras exhibit such precision if they are to be called historians. In antiquity the distinction between mythi-

---

[3] Thucydides 1.97.2 (specifically of Hellanicus' work). In Herodotus 7.96 *historia* is applied to the story told; in Aristotle, *Rhetoric* 1.4 (1360a.36) and *Poetics* 9.3 (1451b.5–7, see below, fn. 5), the term definitely describes the written results of historical inquiry.

cal past and historical past was very often a feeble one; "the Greeks, it has been said, had only historical tragedies," whether the subject was the murder of Agamemnon or the Persian invasion of 480.[4] Although we ourselves may draw a clear line between myth and history, this does not justify the conclusion that any age which could confuse the two was totally lacking in the historical spirit or, alternatively, that myth served in such an age as a completely satisfactory explanation of the past. The argument of this work is intended to show how an attitude which we may properly call historical emerged within a very simple society; but, if we are to find the clues we need, sympathy is demanded, not scorn based on the standards of modern historicism.

To explain the bearing of this comment, the origins and early qualities of Greek civilization must be kept in mind. The beginnings, thus, were humble and obscure. The advanced arts and palace economies of Minoan and Mycenaean times fell as the palaces were burned in the thirteenth and twelfth centuries B.C.; the physical evidence for the Dark Ages which followed, down to 700 B.C., consists of little but vases and a few bronze objects buried with the dead. No major settlements existed, and even villages have not often been found; in some parts of Greece the population, far scantier than earlier, seems to have been nomadic. Only toward 700 B.C. did architecture, sculpture, the working of gold and ivory, and other skills reappear in the Aegean basin.

The Greeks inherited from their past not only poverty as their constant companion but also a primitive pattern of social thought, not all traces of which were gone even by classic times. Peoples on this level are not inclined to view their world historically. They may deny the existence of change, as did one persistent wing of Greek thought which, in philosophy, sought to prove that the eternal was unchanging. If change must be admitted to exist, the source may well be assigned to divine will, another concept long evident in Hel-

[4] F. W. Walbank, *Historia*, IX (1960), p. 225.

8

lenic society. Among the Greeks in particular a rich and plastic imagination created their ever influential mythology as an explanation of the past; this myth-spinning ability rose around and virtually swallowed up even figures of historical times, such as Alexander the Great.

Other inherent qualities of Greek thought reinforced this unhistorical attitude, as incarnated in Homer. The great epics, and also the epic cycle, worked a mighty influence in arts and letters on down into the themes used in red-figured pottery, the odes of Pindar and Bacchylides, and the Attic tragedies which were temporally parallel with the first history; Herodotus himself shows clear effects of the epic outlook and narrative style. When statues labeled Themistocles, Pericles, and other historical personalities were erected in the fifth century, they depicted idealized figures rather than true individuals; the companion drive of Greek philosophy was toward general, not specific, principles.

The Greeks, in sum, began their civilization in an "unhistorical" attitude and experienced continuing pressures toward generalization, toward poetic and imaginative interpretation of events, and toward pure presentism in the violent interactions of their city-states. It is small wonder that the historical outlook awoke only slowly. Even in the fourth century, when history had become a common art, Aristotle could dismiss it with the observation, "Poetry is something more philosophic and of graver import than history, since its statements are of the nature rather of universals, whereas those of history are singulars." [5] Rhetoricians, poets, and statesmen continued to

---

[5] *Poetics* 9.3 (1451b.5–7) (tr. Bywater). Among the many commentaries on this statement see Kurt von Fritz, *Entretiens Hardt*, IV (Geneva, 1956), pp. 115–27; Raymond Weil, *Aristote et l'histoire: essai sur la 'Politique'* (Paris, 1960), pp. 163–78; J. A. O. Larsen, *Classical Philology*, LVII (1962), p. 249, who suggests Aristotle had in mind the raw material of constitutions; but cf. A. W. Gomme, *The Greek Attitude to Poetry and History* (Berkeley, 1954), pp. 1–2 and passim. The difficulty in determining what Aristotle meant—from our point of view— illustrates, incidentally, the semantic and intellectual problem noted earlier in the text.

make use of mythological as well as historical examples; history had little place in education; and even within the realm of historical composition the concept that the truth was all that mattered was rarely the sole guiding light.[6]

Modern students have often magnified the factors just noted so as to reach the sweeping conclusion that the Greeks were *totally* unhistorical. Nietzsche struck this note in his observation, "The Greeks, the famous people of a past still near to us, had the 'unhistorical sense' strongly developed in the period of their greatest power." Later, Spengler bluntly labeled the Greeks "ahistorical"; Collingwood emphasized their "rigorously anti-historical metaphysics"; and Croce, while admitting some sense of history in antiquity, ruthlessly criticized its deficiencies in the field. Recent Christian students of man's progress have simplified the picture by asserting that to the Greeks time was cyclic, while since the Christian revelation it has been a straight line.[7] These views, often fantastic, would be of little moment if they did not carry great weight among general students of historiography and of Western civilization; the recent, provocative study *What Is History?* by E. H. Carr thus asserts that "like the ancient civilizations of Asia, the classical civilization of Greece and Rome was basically unhistorical," though the volume carries on its cover a seated figure labeled Clio.[8]

If the following pages from time to time stress the factors impeding the appearance of a historical outlook among the

---

[6] It should, nonetheless, be noted that the main ancient essay on historical composition which survives, Lucian's *The Way to Write True History*, elevates truth in fact as the prime requisite.

[7] Friedrich Nietzsche, *The Use and Abuse of History* (Indianapolis: Bobbs-Merrill reprint, 1957), p. 24; Oswald Spengler, *Der Untergang des Abendlandes* (abbrev. ed.; Munich, 1959), p. 196; R. G. Collingwood, *The Idea of History* (New York: Galaxy reprint, 1956), pp. 20, 29–30; Benedetto Croce, *Teoria e storia della storiografia* (3d ed.; Bari, 1927), pp. 174ff.; Reinhold Niebuhr, *Faith and History* (New York, 1949), pp. 15–16, 37–41. On Spengler's views, see Eduard Schwartz, "Ueber das Verhältnis der Hellenen zur Geschichte," *Logos*, IX (1920/21), pp. 171–87.

[8] E. H. Carr, *What Is History?* (New York, 1962), p. 145.

Greeks, this represents chiefly an effort to assess scrupulously the varied aspects of Hellenic culture. The rise of history in so difficult a setting was close to a miracle; and the first great history, that of Herodotus, bears within it many marks of his difficulty. Yet the preface of this work is enough to suggest that he *was* writing what we would call history. His outward motive, Herodotus himself states, was to preserve the memory of great deeds; and this function of recording the past for its own sake has always been one of the historian's most obvious tasks. Nonetheless we can see at least dimly in Herodotus—and still more in Thucydides—two other important concepts of history: that the past is different from the present, but real in its own existence; and that the present condition of man, in secular terms, is the product of past human development.

These latter aspects were incompletely sensed in the ancient world, which continued to stress the significance of myth and to believe in divine control. Even so, historians arose from the fifth century onward, generation after generation, down into Byzantine times, to describe to their contemporaries the world in which they lived and, thus, what they themselves were in reality. The volume of historical writing in Greek is testimony that an audience of historical interest demanded this type of explanation of its past and present. In turn, history nourished a humanistic attitude well summed up in Cicero's remark, "to be ignorant of what occurred before you were born is to remain always a child." [9]

[9] Cicero, *Orator* 120.

CHAPTER 1

THE WORLD

OF EPIC AND MYTH

ЛЛЛЛЛЛЛЛЛЛЛЛЛЛЛЛЛЛЛЛЛ

THE HOMERIC EPICS are the fountainhead of that great
stream of development which by the fifth century was to
produce written drama, scientific treatises, philosophy, and
history. The *Iliad* and the *Odyssey* are, to be sure, none of
these. They are poetry, alike in outward form and in inward
spirit. Although a student of modern historiography would
give such material no place, we shall not find it easy to expel
the epics gracefully; for to do so one must give battle to a
determined school which treats them as almost divinely inspired true history.

In reality Homer did not intend to write history; and the
mental attitude exhibited in his tales is far removed from that
of the historian. This conclusion I shall justify below at some
length, for it admirably illustrates the unhistorical inheritance
of later Hellenic thought. But this is not all which one must
say about the epics and their country cousins, the myths. Since
the Greeks did eventually develop a historical outlook, intellectual seeds capable of growth in this direction should also
be lurking in the epic, however inconsistent their presence
may be with its primary character.

Nowadays we can no longer discuss early Greece simply as
the "Homeric age," for the evidence grows that not all the

cultural and economic developments in this era (roughly 1100–700 B.C.) were of purely native Aegean origin. By the eighth century B.C. the Greeks were again in contact with the far more developed Near Eastern societies which had earlier stimulated the Minoan and Mycenaean worlds; that link had been almost shattered during the great upheavals, movements of peoples, and general decline in culture at the end of the second millennium. When the ties were resumed, they drew the Near East and Greece ever closer, and finally the Persian Empire essayed to conquer European Greece—the subject of the first great history written by a Greek. In this chapter, accordingly, we must turn from local Aegean progress to consider also the extent to which the Near East may have offered models in the historical field. This detour will have an unexpected profit as regards the spur which led to historical writing, but the essential roots of Greek historiography will be found to lie within Hellenic civilization.

Nonetheless no history had yet been written in the Aegean world by 700 B.C., the close of the first phase of Greek civilization. In looking at the world of epic and myth, we can easily see why this was so; the Greeks had a long road to traverse in passing from the unhistorical to the historical world.

HOMER AND HISTORY

The *Iliad* and the *Odyssey* were tales laid in a distant past, the era of the Trojan War; this we today consider to have been the late Mycenaean period (the thirteenth century B.C.). Almost everything else in Homeric scholarship has been, and continues to be, the subject of fierce debate. The period, thus, in which the epics were put together in the form in which later ages have known them remains uncertain, for Homeric bards sundered past from present and felt no compulsion to give contemporary references. Much of the material was of

ancient inheritance, and the Homeric dialect and poetic technique were themselves artificial constructions which were elaborated over many generations; a reasonable guess as to the
final crystallization of the epics is that the *Iliad* emerged
shortly before the middle of the eighth century B.C., and the
Odyssey a generation or so later.[1] In this event the two epics
were by different authors, but the similarity in style and
outlook is so great that one may continue to employ the term
"Homer" as a collective noun.

Whenever composed, the Homeric epics were first and last
poetry. Homer certainly felt that the events he recounted had
actually taken place, but his aim was not simply to rehearse
the Trojan War or the travels of Odysseus as recitals of pure
fact. The opening lines of the *Iliad* clearly announce that that
epic will revolve about the wrath of Achilles and the conse-
quences for the Achaean host and, still more, for Achilles
himself. Had the epics been simply historical treatises they
would long since have suffered the fate of those later epics of
the Trojan cycle which did, in a sense, try to historicize the
epic tradition by telling what came before and after the *Iliad*.
But as sympathetic explorations of human character and also
as adventure tales, to say nothing of their purely poetic genius, the *Iliad* and the *Odyssey* have captured the imagination
of generation after generation.

Apart from the obvious fact that Homer was a poet, the
principal proof that he did not intend to write history lies
perhaps in the fact that his stories of the past had no direct
connection with his own world; for an essential ingredient of
the historical outlook is the belief that the past leads into, and
helps determine, the present. But we may go further: the
frame of mind of this early period was not one likely to have

---

[1] Good general introductions to the mass of Homeric scholarship may be
found in Albin Lesky, *History of Greek Literature* (2d ed.; London,
1966), pp. 14–79; John L. Myres, *Homer and His Critics*, ed. Dorothea
Gray (London, 1958); Wolfgang Schadewaldt, *Von Homers Welt und
Werk* (4th ed.; Stuttgart, 1965). For the date advanced above, see
Lesky, pp. 14, 48; Starr, *Origins*, pp. 156–65.

produced a historical narrative, in the sense of a reasoned account of man in time and space.[2] This conclusion rests in part on the general level of society in the Homeric era, a point to which I shall return shortly in connection with the myths; but it can be adequately demonstrated from the evidence of the epics themselves.

As far as space is concerned, Homer knows generally the major districts and sites of the Aegean, sometimes in Mycenaean terms; these appear in the *Iliad* in the extended catalogues of Achaean contingents (2.484–759) and of Trojan allies (2.816–77). But neither directions nor relative locations are very sharply set even within the Aegean, and once Odysseus breaks out of this enclave into the wide Mediterranean we enter with him the realm of fairy tale. Scholars and seamen have tried repeatedly to fit the wanderings of Odysseus to the realities of Mediterranean geography; but the efforts have been faulty in their basic principle. As a careful student of ancient geography sums up Homer's world, "He does what he pleases with a blank."[3] True history, it need scarcely be said, does not operate quite thus with the spatial factor.

Homer's sense of time, again, is subjective rather than historical. Even though events proceed in a generally temporal order during the wrath of Achilles, the reader can never be sure how many days elapse as he moves between Mount Olympus and the plains of Troy. In the *Odyssey* time becomes even more confused as we follow now Telemachus, now Odys-

[2] On Homer and history, see generally Franz Hampl, "Die Ilias ist kein Geschichtsbuch," *Serta philologica Aenipontana*, VII–VIII (1961), pp. 37–63; I have sought to illustrate one specific aspect in which poetic requirements warped objective reality in "Homeric Cowards and Heroes," *The Classical Tradition* (Ithaca, 1966), pp. 58–63. The opposite point of view, however, still holds wide sway; cf. Denys Page, *History and the Homeric Iliad* (Berkeley, 1959).

[3] J. O. Thomson, *History of Ancient Geography* (Cambridge, 1948), p. 27. Eratosthenes (in Strabo 1.2.14 [C23]) had already asserted the irreality of Odyssean wanderings. Cf. the remarks of Rudolf Güngerich, *Die Küstenbeschreibung in der griechischen Literatur* (Münster, 1950), pp. 6–7; and more generally Brigitte Hellwig, *Raum und Zeit im homerischen Epos* (Hildesheim, 1964).

seus, now the suitors in Penelope's palace; it simply does not
unfold in any historical manner. The very word to be used
later for time as an objective phenomenon, *chronos*, has an
impressionistic flavor in Homer: in the *Iliad* it means an
instant, while in the *Odyssey* it more often connotes a duration as an empty, waiting period. More specific, but equally
subjective, is the word for "day," *emar*, which can be the
subject of a sentence (unlike *chronos*); for the term often
carries with it the concept of a destiny fated to a hero such as
Hector at a specific point—though as in the phrase "day of
slavery" the destiny may be an extended one.[4] Homer is aware
that the past, when one man could lift a stone two cannot now
budge, is different from the present; [5] but he has neither any
sense that they are intimately connected nor any desire to
speak of the world about him, save in the general terms of
similes to lions, flocks of geese, and other natural phenomena.
While the seasons revolve about men and Odysseus marks as
an oddity of the island of Calypso that there one does not
know the regions of darkness and dawn, change is not marked
by any clearly conceived yardstick of time.[6] As in space, so in
time the epics float.

Particularly illuminating is Homer's picture of man, for the
deeds of heroes are the very stuff of his poetry.[7] The heroes are

[4] χρόνος: Silvio Accame, "La Concezione del tempo nell'età omerica
ed arcaica," *Rivista di filologia classica*, n.s. XXXIX (1961), pp. 359–94;
Hermann Fränkel, "Die Zeitauffassung in der frühgriechischen Literatur," *Wege und Formen frühgriechischen Denkens* (Munich, 1960),
pp. 1–22. ἦμαρ: Accame, pp. 367–72; R. B. Onians, *The Origins of
European Thought about the Body, the Mind, the Soul, the World,
Time and Fate* (2d ed.; Cambridge, 1954), pp. 411–15; *Odyssey* 9.16ff.
See also Thaddaeus Zielinski, "Die Behandlung gleichzeitiger Ereignisse
im antiken Epos," *Philologus*, Supplementband VIII (1901).
[5] *Iliad* 5.303–4; 12.447–9.
[6] *Odyssey* 10.190–2.
[7] Fränkel, *DuP*, pp. 58–94; Bruno Snell, *The Discovery of the Mind*
(New York: Harper Torchbook, 1960), pp. 1–22, and also "Homer und
die Entstehung des geschichtlichen Bewusstseins bei den Griechen,"
Varia Variorum (Münster-Köln, 1952), pp. 2–12. On human independ-
ence see especially A. Lesky, "Göttliche und menschliche Motivation im
homerischen Epos," *Sitzungsberichte der Heidelberger Akademie,*

individualized, though we do not know their physical appearance. They act, and their actions are carefully described; indeed, they exist only in action inasmuch as they have no inner, reflective self-consciousness. To explore Homeric psychology at length would carry us far afield into a tangle of complexities; for the epics provide the first literary expression of a realm of ill-defined and jarring concepts which had a great potential. The heroes do somehow possess freedom of will to act as they wish, subject to taking the penalties the gods may inflict. Yet far more evident at this early state is the belief that deeds are divinely inspired.

As I shall have occasion to argue more fully later, a truly historical outlook can coexist with the concept that the ultimate responsibility for men's actions lies with the gods or with God; but men must, in such a case, move themselves at least immediately. In the Homeric epics the gods do not simply pass decrees on Mount Olympus; they come down and talk to Achilles or take human form to mislead Hector to his death. More generally, any Homeric hero who engages in unusual behavior can be said to be directed by his *ate*, or divine possession; or to do a great deed by reason of his *menos*, divine power. His *moira*, or fate, is a matter determined by the gods or by an impersonal force above and behind them.[8] The greatness of poetic insight and warm compassion which produced the *Iliad* and the *Odyssey* created masterful human portraits, canonical examples to later Greece; but Homer moved unconsciously, in a deeply religious spirit, to explain the modes of operation of his heroes. Rational historical reflection we should not perhaps expect in

---

phil.-hist. Klasse, 1961.IV; Ernst Wüst, "Von den Anfängen des Problems der Willensfreiheit," *Rheinisches Museum*, CI (1958), pp. 75–91.
[8] W. C. Greene, *Moira* (Cambridge, Mass., 1944); U. Bianchi, ΔΙΟΣ ΑΙΣΑ (Rome, 1953); E. Leitzke, *Moira und Gottheit im alten homerischen Epos* (Göttingen, 1930). In the *Odyssey* men begin to draw apart from the world about them as something distinct (see Fränkel, *DuP*, pp. 94–103).

a poet; still, in reading the epics one does not sense that deliberate analysis of human nature was a tool anywhere available within this simple world.

In poetic techniques, true, Homer operated on very refined, stylized principles. The Homeric hexameter is basically a simple line, but its variations are skillfully marshaled to create a flowing, artistic work of great length, just as eighth-century potters at Athens decorated the majestic Dipylon vases five and six feet high with a limited number of motifs (see Plate I). Many generations of past bards had created a stock of standardized epithets or descriptive phrases, and had elaborated the deeds of the heroes in shorter works which modern scholars seek, in acrimonious debate, to extract from the text of our present poems. Yet this stylization and standardization combine to weaken the possibility that Homer could have written historically, had he wished; for even individual duels are cast in a generalized mold, which eliminates the unique particularity of historical reality. Here we approach one of the enduring qualities of the Greek outlook which was to cause difficulty in applying a thoroughgoing historical perspective; true history moves always from specific happenings.

The view of Homer advanced in the preceding paragraphs I have intentionally sharpened, for recently there has been a ground swell of scholarly willingness once again to credit the Homeric epics as "historical documents." Similar enthusiasm attends efforts to extract nuggets of historical value from the myths, which stand on a lower plane of artistic development than the epics but obey much the same principles of thought; some students go so far as virtually to assert that the intent of epic poets and tellers of myth was to preserve historical information. So archaeologists relate the later building stages of Mycenae with the myths of the Perseids and Atreids; historians recount the early history of Attica in terms of the Theseus legends; whole volumes, apparently sturdy and detailed in their text, will be found, upon inspecting the footnotes, to rest on gossamer spun out of legend and the weakest of tradition.[9]

This credulity represents in part a reaction against the hypercriticism of the late nineteenth century. Of late it has been nourished by the discovery that the Mycenaean tablets were written in Greek, but essentially it links onto the ancient belief in the literal truth of epic and myth. Particularly in Hellenistic times myths were quarried and manipulated to justify current political or cultural attitudes and claims; a famous relief of the Apotheosis of Homer, probably carved in the late third or early second century B.C., surrounds Homer with various figures including a youth labeled *Mythos* and a female figure inscribed *Historia,* to suggest that both were included in his work.[1]

Here we might take warning from the earliest real historians of Greece itself. Undoubtedly they were inclined to accept epic and myth as being real testimony of the past; after all it was the only evidence (apart from Cyclopean walls) transmitted to them from earlier times. Yet they knew that this sort of past was timeless, that it could not be linked to the present; and when they approached it, they did so with an unconscious caution which reveals their different, basically historical attitude. Herodotus evidently felt that he could trust memories only for the past two or three generations, for his account rarely reached back farther than the mid-sixth century. He cited Homer on occasion, but almost never to prove the truth of an early event; on the contrary he asserted that Homer or some other poet invented the name of Ocean and

[9] George Mylonas, *Mycenae and the Mycenaean Age* (Princeton, 1966); N. G. L. Hammond, *History of Greece to 322 B.C.* (Oxford, 1959), p. 68; G. L. Huxley, *Early Sparta* (Cambridge, Mass., 1962). Cf. my review of the latter in *American Journal of Philology,* LXXXVI (1965), pp. 110–12; and further criticism of these unsound attitudes in "La Storia greca arcaica: saggio sul metodo di recostruzione," *Rivista di filologia,* 3. ser. XCII (1964), pp. 5–23; "The Credibility of Early Spartan History," *Historia,* XIV (1965), pp. 257–72.
[1] Gisela M. A. Richter, *Portraits of the Greeks* (London, 1965), p. 54.

altered the story of Helen for poetic reasons. Thucydides was more inclined to accept epic and myth, though only after he had rationalized it; but twice in his opening sections he found it difficult to accept details on Homer's authority. The use of mythological examples to prove a point, to warn, or to draw a lesson was already well established in Homeric times, and remained one of the major characteristics of poetry and oratory thereafter; still, Aristotle felt a certain uneasiness in the matter when he advised orators to use historical examples as really having happened.[2]

To return to Homer, it is likely that some kind of attack on Troy took place long before; and an inherited matrix of poetic invention and elaboration about the event was so set in Homer's day that he was not free to create his epic tales *ad libidem*. Nonetheless, as one investigates the evolution of the *Chanson de Roland* or the *Nibelungenlied*—to cite two parallels from more literate ages—one cannot feel that the equally long gestation of the Homeric epics, in an illiterate period, produced in the end anything very close to real events.

The question, however, as to the degree to which the *Iliad* preserved the memory of an actual Trojan War is a red herring. What is really significant in the present connection is the problem whether Homer intended to write history. As I have already suggested, any effort to answer this issue affirmatively seems to me both to warp the nature of history itself and to slur his poetic genius; his own works carry within them the disproof of the proposition. To broaden out the grounds on which a proper judgment can be made, let us set Homer within the Dark Ages proper.

[2] Herodotus: 2.23 and 2.116; in 4.29 he quotes *Odyssey* 4.85 for a natural fact, and in 7.161.3 the Athenians seek to use Homer as evidence. In his long work, though, Herodotus cites Homer only ten times. Thucydides: 1.9.4, 1.10.3. Fourth century: Aristotle, *Rhetoric* 2.20 (1394a.7–8); Ephorus, *FGrH*, no. 70, F 9. See Robert Oehler, *Mythologische Exempla in der älteren griechischen Dichtung* (Aarau, 1923); Jaeger, *Paideia*, I, pp. 52–71; M. I. Finley, "Myth, Memory, and History," *History and Theory*, IV (1965), pp. 281–302.

That this was a simple world is shown by the scanty archaeological material of the period as well as by Homer's own description of the ways of life of his heroes. Earlier in the Dark Ages some great sites such as Corinth had even been deserted for a time; others, like Argos and Athens, had been continuously inhabited, but only by agricultural villages. Down to almost the end of the eighth century religious shrines were tiny huts; the working of figures in clay or bronze was by this date just passing beyond the rudely conventional into more consciously conceived small sculptures. Society was rigidly structured; anyone cast out by his local group was without public protection, an outlaw who had to beg the support of some foreign war chief.[3] A modern observer, thrown back suddenly into this world, would feel himself in an utterly primitive land.

If we are to hope to understand how Homer and his contemporaries might have thought about "history," we must not bring with us that attitude which Reinhold Niebuhr sums up,

> In modern culture both time and history are regarded as self-explanatory. They do not require explanation but become the principle of explanation by which life is given meaning.[4]

This is an advanced concept, as can be shown by several independent lines of evidence. Children, for example, do not appear to grasp the irreversibility of time until they are about five years old; only thereafter do they gain a sense of continuity. In one African country today the natives are described as lacking a time sense; "they live in the time they have, and do not count it." One of the most provocative and stimulating studies of this problem in early societies, Mircea Eliade's *Myth of the Eternal Return,* may go too far in asserting that "Archaic man . . . tends to set himself in opposition, by every means in his power, to history, regarded as a succession of

[3] Starr, *Origins,* pp. 77–186.
[4] *Faith and History* (New York, 1949), p. 37.

events that are irreversible, unforeseeable, possessed of autonomous value"; [5] but his analysis of primitive levels of thought skillfully demonstrates that men have not always automatically visualized their past and present in really historical terms.

Only against this background can one hope to assess the bearing of Homer and the myths with respect to history; Homer's views of space, time, and the nature of man, as molded by his poetic genius within a stylized framework, have only an ancestral relationship with those of true history, which appeared centuries later in Hellenic development. In Greek myth, again, events take place in a world which has its own space and time. In this matter there is no need for elaborate demonstration and quotation of mythical examples, which will come easily to anyone's mind; what does deserve note is the fact that mythical remembrancers were far less bound by form than were the epic poets. Accordingly their tales could evolve and change over the generations, and so it is the more significant that the earliest discernible levels of mythology, especially those connected with Heracles, are as unhistorical in nature as are the Homeric epics. [6]

There is, then, no reason to expect that the Greeks who lived in the undeveloped society of the Dark Ages, 1100–700, were historically conscious unless one yields uncritical adherence to that ever persuasive tendency to idealize the Homeric

[5] Mircea Eliade, *Cosmos and History: The Myth of the Eternal Return* (New York: Harper Torchbook, 1959), p. 95; Martha Gelhorn, *Atlantic Monthly*, September 1963, p. 42, of Tanganyika; Ph. Malrieu, "Aspects sociaux de la construction du temps chez l'enfant," *Journal de psychologie*, LIII (1956), pp. 315–32, whose remarks may be complemented by Paul Fraisse, *Psychologie du temps* (Paris, 1957), esp. pp. 149ff., 257ff.; see also François Chatelet, *La Naissance de l'histoire* (Paris, 1962), pp. 402–3.
[6] B. A. van Groningen, *In the Grip of the Past* (Leiden, 1953), pp. 100–3. Specific examples may be found in Hans Herter, "Theseus der Athener," *Rheinisches Museum*, LXXXVIII (1939), pp. 244–86, 289–326; M. P. Nilsson, *Cults, Myths, Oracles and Politics in Ancient Greece* (Lund, 1951); John Forsdyke, *Greece before Homer: Ancient Chronology and Mythology* (London, 1957).

world as the forerunner of classical civilization. Nor was the era itself likely to have produced contemporary history or even historical records. Down into the eighth century the Greek world was an amorphous mass of peoples (*ethnoi*), whose leaders, the kings (*basileis*), were little more than military chieftains. Hunting, cattle raiding, tilling the fields, and listening to the bards—these were the occupations of life; not until the city-state arose were there to be conscious internal conflicts or external aggrandizements which could provide the spur to historical records and memories.

LEGACY OF MYTH AND EPIC

From the point of view of the present investigation, the main legacy of myth and epic to later centuries may be taken as a fundamentally unhistorical attitude. For centuries to come the deeds of the Olympian deities and of heroes such as Heracles, Theseus, or figures of the Trojan War were the main stuff of art and literature. The generalized, idealized mode of treatment which commonly prevailed accords completely with Eliade's picture of "the archaic mentality, which cannot accept what is individual and preserves only what is exemplary." [7]

Yet it will not do to take the next step with Eliade and call this mentality, in its Greek form, *anti*-historical. To Eliade a major device by which a society of this persuasion breaks loose from history is the creation of a myth of an eternally dying and reviving god whom the society celebrates in festivals of re-creation. Corroboration for the scheme has been sought in the Cretan belief that Zeus died each year or in the annual festivals of Dionysus; Gilbert Murray even sought to explain the rise of tragedy as connected with the Year-spirit (*Eniau-*

[7] *Cosmos and History,* p. 44.

tos-Daimon). Murray's views have gained little credence, nor is there genuine support for the theory of Eliade as far as Greece is concerned if we examine the main lines of its intellectual and religious concepts. On the contrary seeds of a potentially historical spirit may be found in that body of epic and myth which we have thus far considered in its nonhistorical aspects.

A few examples will suffice to suggest this other side. One requirement of history, for instance, is respect for the evidence, a requirement which certainly lay heavily on Homer; as a *rhapsode* he stitched together inherited materials, and his warrior audience gave him little freedom with which to invent anew as far as the "facts" of the tale were concerned. The past of which he chanted had no direct connection with the present in which he and his auditors lived, but toward its great heroes he maintained an objective approach, a fundamental prerequisite for later historical attitudes.[8] Objectivity, however, need not entail the loss of sympathy for the men who struggle and eventually die—and this quality, together with an underlying optimism, pervades the epic portrayal. Soon, as we shall see below, there came the second great poet of early Greece, Hesiod, who was to construct a scheme of successive races moving from the golden and silver through that of heroes into the present age of iron; and even the myths which the Greeks told to themselves to account for their background had a fundamentally logical, nonmagical, and sequential quality. Theories of direct opposition to history, as an irreversible flow of events, will not fit Greek thought from its earliest visible level onward, though much had still to be achieved before a truly historical attitude could emerge.

In other ways as well the inheritance from epic and myth

[8] Respect for the evidence: Harald Patzer, "'Ραψῳδός," *Hermes*, LXXX (1952), pp. 314–25; Fränkel, *DuP*, pp. 64–75; Gomme, *Greek Attitude to Poetry and History*, pp. 2–41. Objectivity: Gomme, pp. 42–8; Aubrey de Selincourt, *The World of Herodotus* (London, 1962), p. 292, observes "Homer does not blame the folly of men; he does not try to *argue them different* any more than Herodotus does."

favored, or directed, that emergence. Alike in epic, in the myths, and in the pottery of the eighth century high gifts of logical order and analysis are reflected, if still perhaps unconsciously.[9] The epics, again, provided models of extended narrative, cast in supple language, in which the heroes were portrayed dramatically and, as it were, "in the round" rather than as puppets on a screen; what happened to them must be explained, its significance adumbrated. Above all, the *Iliad* and the *Odyssey* dealt with men, moved no doubt by the gods, yet somehow possessed of human passions, ambitions, and sensitivities; the man-centered quality of Greek civilization begins, for us, in Homer but soon manifests itself in the arts of the age of expansion. When the first student of man's history, Herodotus, appeared, his major single model was Homer.

CONTRIBUTIONS OF THE NEAR EAST

Epic and myth sum up the literary inheritance from the earliest, formative stage of Greek civilization, but this is not the only strand which helped to shape the Hellenic future. The Near East had had civilized centers in Egypt and Mesopotamia since the fourth millennium B.C. and had never, even in the worst of the invasions and upheavals at the close of the Bronze Age, quite lost the tissue of ordered political, religious, and cultured life. During the eighth century the Assyrian imperialists united much of it politically, and a cultural *koine* became evident which had strong influence as far as Etruscan Italy; the Greeks were in contact with this polished society well before 700.[1] Among the most crucial questions in the rise of Greek civilization are the extent to which the Aegean drew

[9] Cf. my discussion of the pottery in *Origins*, pp. 99–103, 148–56.
[1] On the resumption of contacts see T. J. Dunbabin, *The Greeks and their Eastern Neighbours* (London, 1957); Santo Mazzarino, *Fra Oriente e Occidente* (Florence, 1947); Starr, *Origins*, pp. 189–220, with references to the archaeological literature.

upon the far more developed world to its east and the manner in which Greek culture transmuted its borrowings.

If the Near East had a sense of history—a doubtful possibility in most areas—it does not follow that the Greeks borrowed thence a mature, ordered concept of historical composition. On this aspect we may be brief inasmuch as significant debate which bears on our subject arises only in two areas, those of Hebrew historiography and a possible Persian influence on Herodotus. Yet a neat paradox emerges when one considers the relations of the Aegean and the Near East: while the Greek form of history owed nothing to Eastern models, the Greeks would not have written history had they not been in contact with the states and cultures of the Levant.

First, Near Eastern historiography proper; and here the modern historian is likely to think of that remarkable variety of records on which we can draw today to form a fairly continuous account of the progress of Near Eastern states over millennia. There are treaties, as between Ramses II of Egypt and the Hittite Hattusilis III;[2] state correspondence; complaints and petitions; and many other forms of documentary evidence. Such materials, however, were not intended to be formal accounts of present and past events; for these we must look elsewhere.

In Egypt lists of kings were kept from the Old Kingdom onward; genealogies of priests, such as the Memphite priests of Ptah, also existed. For the height of New Kingdom militarism, the middle and later centuries of the second millennium B.C., the temples of Karnak, Medinet Habu, and elsewhere display great reliefs of the royal victories with hieroglyphic texts providing details of the number of enemy killed, beasts seized, and so on; private tombs recount the deeds of the generals and administrators of Pharaoh. From the contempo-

---

[2] *Ancient Near East Texts Relating to the Old Testament,* ed. James B. Pritchard (Princeton, 1950), pp. 199–203 (Egyptian and Hittite versions—not quite in agreement); cf. his valuable collection of historical texts, pp. 227ff.

rary Hittite world survive an account of the accession to power of king Hattusilis III and what may be called chronicles of events. Omen lists and annual chronicles preserve many details of the rise of the Assyrian Empire, the wars of which are depicted in the graphic reliefs of Khorsabad and Nineveh.[3]

To call this varied corpus "history" is rather difficult. Although lists of kings and eponymous magistrates from Egypt and Mesopotamia show a sense of continuity, as well as being practically useful, in themselves they are not history. The decorations of temple walls or the erection of steles within the temples are essentially an accounting to the gods for their earthly favors to the rulers. Even the Assyrian annals, which are the fullest such records, are primarily of this class. In assessing Near Eastern historical materials we must distinguish sharply between their historical utility to modern students and the intent of their composers; in "secular" reports as a whole it is difficult to see more than vainglorious boasting or gratitude to divine patrons. A sober desire to describe the past analytically does not appear, for the accounts of the origins of the world in various lands, which come the closest, are couched always in mythical terms.

In only one case can this view be seriously questioned, that of the Hebrew historical books embraced in the Old Testament. Modern students of historiography commonly find themselves embarrassed to assess this material because of its strongly theological twist—Collingwood, for one, simply lumps it with the theocratic records of Mesopotamia and Egypt.[4]

[3] See generally the excellent collection of essays in *Idea of History in the Ancient Near East,* ed. Robert C. Dentan (New Haven, 1955); Burr C. Brundage, "The Birth of Clio: A Résumé and Interpretation of Ancient Near Eastern Historiography," *Teachers of History* (Ithaca, 1954), pp. 199–230; James T. Shotwell, *The Story of Ancient History* (New York: Columbia paperback, 1961), pp. 74–103. On the Hittite records see also O. R. Gurney, *The Hittites* (London, 1952), pp. 175–6.
[4] Collingwood, *The Idea of History,* p. 17. See the essay by Millar Burrows, "Ancient Israel," *Idea of History in the Ancient Near East,* pp.

This will not do; the intent to show divine providence working its will in earthly events was strong in Hebrew historiography, but a great deal of undeniably historical writing in more recent times has still attributed the ultimate impetus of human life to divine will. However much later scribes revised and reworked the early records of Israel, the fundamental core was historical, as in the almost contemporary and remarkable account of David in II Samuel 9–20. David, Solomon, and a host of other Hebrew figures really lived, and the intervention of Yahweh does not totally disguise their earthly life.

A challenging book in comparison of Hebrew and Greek thought by Thorleif Boman has recently gone so far as to argue that the Hebrew outlook was the one which was dynamic and temporally oriented and that the Greek was static and spatial.[5] To reach this conclusion, on the Greek side, Boman takes the dangerous if well-trodden path of relying almost solely on Plato; the philosopher Heraclitus, who argued that all was change, must accordingly be un-Greek, perhaps even a Near Easterner. Worse yet, Boman's argument overlooks the development of an impersonal, quantitative sense of time in Greek thought. That there were unhistorical tendencies in Hellas we have already noticed and shall consider again; but Boman's arbitrary comparisons do not quite account for the fact that the Greeks also developed *the* historic spirit of later Western civilization.

His treatment of the Hebrew side can also be faulted; yet in the end there is merit in Boman's distinction between a society which thinks causally and looks backward in time—the

---

101–31; Gerhard von Rad, "Der Anfang der Geschichtsschreibung im alten Israel," *Archiv für Kulturgeschichte*, XXXII (1944), pp. 1–42.
[5] Thorleif Boman, *Hebrew Thought Compared with Greek* (Philadelphia, 1960), pp. 51–2, 170; and also E. von Dobschütz, "Zeit und Raum im Denken des Urchristentums," *Journal of Biblical Literature*, XLI (1922), pp. 212–23. Accame, *Rivista di filologia*, n.s. XXXIX (1961), pp. 391–3, is justly critical; as is also Momigliano, *Rivista storica italiana*, LXXIV (1962), pp. 603–7; and *History and Theory*, Beiheft VI (1966), pp. 1ff. On the Hebrew side see also J. Barr, *Biblical Words for Time* (London, 1962).

Greek—and a theologically oriented outlook which views the world teleologically and looks forward in history. From late Hellenistic times onward the Hebrew inheritance was to have ever greater attention until the Christian synthesis of Hebrew and Greek views was perfected. This development came much later; for our present concern the important fact is that, even if the Hebrews wrote history from the beginning of the first millennium onward, it had no influence on the formative period of Greek historical thought. No direct contact between Hebrew and Hellene has yet been shown for this early era, and the fundamental principles of Hebrew historical thought were "incommensurable with Greek historiography." [6]

Nor can one see that the propensities elsewhere in the Near East to make lists of rulers, to set up pious records of royal achievements, or to create romances attributed to real characters had any serious weight in Greek thinking. Eventually the Greeks too were to draw up lists of Athenian archons, priestesses of Hera at Argos, kings of Sparta, and so on, but it appears unlikely that they did so under outside impulse; nor did Greek history begin with the initial step of writing annals. Near Eastern theological schemes of the past of earth and man, as in the story of the Garden of Eden or the theory that all life originated in water, were occasionally drawn upon in Greece; Hesiod, toward the end of the eighth century, knew a little about some Near Eastern myths, which appear in Greek guise in his *Theogony*.[7] He also picked up a concept of man's past as falling into distinct stages; but this idea, perhaps the prime suggestion of early Greek indebtedness to Near Eastern thought, belongs more in the realm of incipient philosophical speculation than to that of history proper.

Some effort, nonetheless, has been made to assert a significant indebtedness of Herodotus to Persian tales. That the Father of History made use of a Persian list of satraps and of Egyptian inscriptions, as far as they were translated for him, is

[6] Momigliano, *Studies in Historiography*, p. 115.
[7] Starr, *Origins*, p. 166.

29

patent; but he goes further by parading Persian sources for the tales of woman-stealing between Asia and Europe with which his history commences. Whether Herodotus was serious in this proemium, designed to gain attention, is more than doubtful; in any case, as one thoughtful critic has noted, the political opposition between the two continents here evident could scarcely have emerged before Herodotus' own lifetime and is much more likely to be of Greek than of Persian origin.[8] Even though fact and romantic tale in his manifold recountal may occasionally have had Eastern origins, we shall find it sensible to conclude that the pattern of the first Greek history is Hellenic when we return to Herodotus in Chapter VI, after surveying the developments of archaic Greece.

The idea of history, as the Greeks were to develop it, had no intrinsic connection with the Near East; but the paradox advanced at the beginning of this section still remains—Herodotus' history could never have been written if the Near East had not existed. Thence came, in the first place, a vital mechanical tool, the alphabet.[9] The Mycenaean world had used a syllabic script, which died out as the palace economies of that era dissolved; across the Dark Ages the Aegean was illiterate until at some point, probably the early eighth century or late in the ninth, a voyager to the Syrian coast picked up and brought back the Phoenician alphabet. Although the names and, largely, the shapes of the individual letters remained Phoenician, the Greeks introduced signs for vowels,

[8] G. de Sanctis, *Studi di storia della storiografia greca* (Florence, 1951), p. 63. The principal argument for Persian influence is Karl Reinhardt, "Herodots Persergeschichten," reprinted in *Herodot*, pp. 320–69, criticized by Harder, ibid., p. 374. Cf. A. Momigliano, "Fattori orientali della storiografia ebraica post-esilica e della storiografia greca," *Rivista storica italiana*, LXXVII (1965), pp. 456–64.
[9] Lillian H. Jeffery, *Local Scripts of Archaic Greece* (Oxford, 1961). Beside the Dipylon jug of the earlier eighth century we now have an alphabetic graffito on a sherd from Gordion "perhaps (conservatively) as early as the first half of the eighth century" according to R. S. Young, *American Journal of Archaeology*, LXX (1966), p. 276.

and so made the alphabet a supple tool for writing poetry; the Homeric epics must thus have been set down not long after their final formulation. When prose appeared, as in treaties and public records, it too could be written without serious difficulty—and read by the growingly literate upper classes of the Greek states. Despite the fact that the Chinese were able to develop history in a cumbrous script, the presence and ever greater use of the alphabet must have facilitated the rise of Greek history as of science and philosophy.

In the second place the venerable, massive monuments and evolved societies of the Near East awakened in the simple Greeks, who came to Syria and Egypt in ever greater numbers, two great streams of thought which led on to more conscious historical meditation. Full consideration of this important aspect must be reserved for the next chapter, but here two specific figures may serve as brief illustration. Hecataeus, standing in front of a long array of wooden statues of past Theban priests, represents one side of this meditation, which spurred the Greeks to visualize earlier times as long and historical; [1] Herodotus, busily noting his impressions of alien peoples on his wide travels, suggests the other aspect.

Homer had drawn little cultural or racial distinction between Trojans and Greeks; in his time, observes Thucydides, "the Hellenes were not yet known by one name, and so marked off as something separate from the outside world." [2] This very comment throws into relief the distinction which was evident by Thucydides' own day, the late fifth century; actually awareness of difference between East and West and therewith a deeper comprehension of the basic unity of Hellenic culture grew steadily across the period 700–500. An almost inevitable historical question to follow was the source of the difference, a problem which rose into real significance once the Greeks and Persians were thrown into extensive,

[1] Herodotus 2.143.
[2] Thucydides 1.3 (tr. Warner).

hostile contact. Both the travels of Herodotus and the history which ensued can be understood only in terms of this awareness.

THE LATER EIGHTH CENTURY

The Greek world was steadily moving toward a great explosion in the decades just on either side of 700, which was to throw Greeks over almost all the shores of the Mediterranean and to produce, in a rush, large-scale sculpture, temples, lyric poetry, and the more conscious, tighter organization of the city-state. Homer composed his epics before this tremendous upheaval; the next great figure in Greek literature lived during the most critical era, but so much to one side that he does not fully reflect all its aspects.

This was Hesiod of Ascra, a village overlooking the Boeotian plain. Since the poet journeyed to Chalcis to commemorate the death of a king for whom there is other evidence, we can place him at just about 700; but in his use of the epic hexameter and in his general cast of thought Hesiod has always been properly linked with Homer rather than with the lyric poets of the next century. Besides a great volume of poetry surviving only in fragments, and not likely to be Hesiod's own works, two major poems bear his name, the *Works and Days* and the *Theogony;* these furnish intriguing evidence which sometimes accords with that of Homer and sometimes stands sharply distinct.

The *Works and Days* is one of the most fascinating and amazing products of all Greek literature. When Hesiod's father died, his elder, wicked brother Perses conspired with the "bribe-swallowing *basileis*" to take most of the inheritance; Hesiod, inspired to poetry by the Muses of his native Helicon, responded with a lengthy exhortation against injustice. The cause of the poem is a specific, real event of the present day, not a legendary tale. Also un-Homeric is Hesiod's effort to explain the injustice of the contemporary world, the origins of which he sought in the past. First he recounts the myth of Pandora, sent by Zeus to plague man for having gained the boon of fire; but next he gives an alternative explanation, that mankind has passed through five successive races—those of gold, of silver, of bronze, of the heroes, and now of iron, "and men never rest from labor and sorrow by day, and from perishing by night." [3]

The concept of races Hesiod probably borrowed from the Near East; but he altered it to accord with the reality, as epic told him, of an age of heroes, "nobler and more righteous, a god-like race of hero-men who are called demi-gods, the race before our own." [4] The generations of man are discontinuous, rather than intimately connected; and modern men, accustomed to ideas of progress, may feel Hesiod has turned the past upside down. Nonetheless the concept of connection between past and present is clearly present in the *Works and Days;* and in view of a common misconception of Greek ideas of time let me emphasize that Hesiod views progress (or deterioration) as essentially on a straight line, not in a cycle.

Apart from its inception in a real event and the theory of human stages, however, Hesiod's *Works and Days* reveals almost as unhistorical an attitude as do the Homeric epics. The source is a real event; and Hesiod fiercely distinguishes true from false.[5] Yet he gives no details of his lawsuit with Perses, and swiftly rises to a plane of generalization about the

---

[3] *Works and Days* 176–7. On Hesiod, see K. von Fritz et al., *Entretiens Hardt VII: Hésiode et son influence* (Geneva, 1960): Friedrich Solmsen, *Hesiod and Aeschylus* (Ithaca, 1949); H. T. Wade-Gery, "Hesiod," *Phoenix*, III (1949), pp. 81–93.
[4] *Works and Days* 158–60. Cf. T. G. Rosenmeyer, "Hesiod and Historiography," *Hermes*, LXXXV (1957), pp. 257–85; J. P. Vernant, "Le mythe hésiodique des races," *Revue de l'histoire des religions*, CLVII (1960), pp. 21–54.
[5] See generally W. Luther, *"Wahrheit" und "Lüge" im ältesten Griechentum*, Diss. Göttingen (Leipzig, 1935), pp. 123–33.

causes and results of injustice; for Zeus will punish the evil and reward the good. From this he passes to a manual on agricultural life (the "works") and then to a mass of magical wisdom on good and bad days in the month. Hesiod knows and describes the seasons; he divides man's life into five stages; he even gives the name of one month (Lenaion); but his poem has little sense of time in general. The word *chronos* appears only once.[6]

Early in the subsequent poem, the *Theogony*, the Muses of Helicon tell Hesiod that "we know how to speak many false things as though they were true; but we know, when we will, to utter true things," a slighting allusion presumably to the Homeric epics.[7] Then they give the poet "a divine voice to celebrate things that shall be and things that were aforetime," which he proceeds to employ for over a thousand lines to chronicle the generations of the gods from Chaos onward, together with the birth of Earth, Hills, Heaven, Ocean, and other physical features. Recent students of Greek philosophy have emphasized the significance of this first study in cosmogony, basically rational in presentation, ordering ancestral myth systematically; for history its significance must lie in the emphasis upon continuity of development in the past to produce the world which Hesiod's contemporaries saw.

Neither in Homer nor in Hesiod can we detect a consciously historical attitude. If anything, our search through the epics, myth, and Hesiod must suggest how difficult it would be for the Greeks, inclined to idealize and to explain the world by divine intervention on every level from the Muses of a moun-

---

[6] Line 326. Observe, though, that Hesiod senses before and after in line 175 and feels that the future results from man's own acts (182ff., 225ff.), though Zeus is also responsible (280ff.).

[7] *Theogony* 27–8. Cf K. von Fritz, "Das Prooemium der hesiodischen Theogonie," *Festschrift Bruno Snell* (Munich, 1956), pp. 29–45; H. Diller, "Hesiod und die Anfänge der griechischen Philosophie," *Antike und Abendland*, II (1946), pp. 140–51; Olof Gigon, *Der Ursprung der griechischen Philosophie: von Hesiod bis Parmenides* (Basel, 1945), pp. 13ff.

tain to the gods of Mount Olympus, to develop a historical spirit.

Often the visual impact of artistic evidence best throws into salient relief major qualities of Greek civilization; and in concluding the necessarily complicated argument of this chapter I would invite a glance at the simple scene shown on Plate I, from the great Dipylon amphora in the National Museum, Athens. Here the corpse lies on its funeral couch with coverlet displayed above; wife and child stand at the head, friends and relatives raise their hands in grief while musicians accompany their wails, and the warriors are at the far left, poised to take away the bier. Although the event is real, we neither know the name of the dead man nor have any clues as to his historical position; the painter of this scene certainly could not have thought in the manner of the sculptors of Trajan's Column or of Meissonier's battle paintings. At this very time Assyrian sculptors were depicting the glories of their warlords; but the Attic potter knows nothing of such Near Eastern achievements.

Yet the artist is saying something which has significance:

> Viewed as a rendering of life it is a solemn scene reduced to its barest terms, terms telling from their very bareness. Here is an artist who has not attempted more than he could exactly perform; an art not childish, but planned and austere.[8]

The remarks could fit Homer as well; artist and poet alike come from a simple world, but both suggest the great possibilities latent within the Hellenic pattern of thought. Man and his deeds are at the center, though as yet conceived almost abstractly. When finally the expanding Greek world had developed more conscious ideas of space and time and had evolved a political framework which spurred, even demanded, historical accounts of the past, these drew primarily, in their

[8] J. D. Beazley, *The Development of Attic Black-figure* (Berkeley, 1951), p. 3. The vase is Athens CC 200; bibliography is given in Starr, *Origins,* pp. 151–2.

ultimate root, from the native Aegean development of the Dark Ages. To return to the visual level, one need only compare the scenes of Plate I and of Plate VI, from the mid-fifth century; both have the same theme, though the later example is far more specific, conscious, and immediately comprehensible.

CHAPTER 2

THE EXPANSION

OF GREECE

ᒧᒐᒧᒐᒧᒐᒧᒐᒧᒐᒧᒐᒧᒐᒧᒐᒧᒐᒧᒐᒧᒐᒧᒐᒧᒐᒧᒐᒧᒐ

To JUDGE from Homer, Hesiod, and Geometric pottery the main qualities of Greek civilization had already made their appearance during the Dark Ages. Next came an explosion in a few decades on either side of 700 B.C. and then a period of sweeping expansion, which had wide effects socially, politically, and intellectually. The era from 700 to 500 B.C., often termed the archaic age as an extension of its major artistic style, will demand our attention for the next four chapters.

The inward marks of change included men's growing self-awareness. Among many thinkers and politicians the result was a bold venturesomeness and almost limitless confidence in human abilities; but this reaction, while significant, was not the only motive force in the thought of the archaic period. Others feared divine retribution for the overgreat pride of mankind; poets and lawgivers alike manifested deep concern at the social oppression and instability of life which marked this age of turmoil and upheaval as the more advanced parts of Greece broke out of the old, traditional ways.[1] Normally a basic optimism checked unreasoning panic, even though poets

[1] E. R. Dodds, *The Greeks and the Irrational* (Berkeley, 1951); Starr, *Origins*, pp. 277-92.

and philosophers felt driven to brood insistently on the place of mankind. One fruit was a conscious analysis of man's own nature and that of the universe about him—and therewith meditation on how both had come to be as they were.

Partly to contain and to channel the political and social alterations the *polis,* or city-state, emerged rather suddenly just before 700 and developed across the age of expansion as the political, religious, and social frame of life. Other outward tokens of change included the rise of a consciously aristocratic way of life; the great growth of trade and industry at home, which produced real urban centers; a wave of overseas colonization; and that efflorescence of arts and letters which we call archaic in sculpture and lyric in poetry.

The literature of the period admirably mirrors its swirling currents. One great influence poured down out of the past, for the Homeric epics were not forgotten. Rather they spread generally during this era over the Aegean world, a process reflected in the decoration of pottery, shield bands, and other artistic media. Alongside the *Iliad* and *Odyssey* there arose new epics of the Trojan cycle, as well as the Theban epics, tales of Heracles' adventures, and the *Homeric Hymns;* these newer stories, composed after 700 B.C., served even more often than Homer's own epics as artistic sources.[2]

The conservative tendency which is visible here appears also in the persistence of Geometric pottery styles. It requires emphasis, for too often we tend to treat Hellenic progress as a uniform, optimistic march from height to height, forgetting the laggards, the recalcitrants, and the self-willed who went by other paths. Still, those poets who wrote anonymously in hexameters did not constitute the dominant wave. In the age of expansion men moved from impersonal epic to highly personal lyric and elegiac verse, in a break as abrupt as that which sundered archaic from classic at the end of the period;

[2] E. Kunze, *Archaische Schildbänder* (Berlin, 1950), pp. 139–73; Dunbabin, *Greeks and their Eastern Neighbours,* pp. 77–87; E. A. Lane, *Annual of the British School at Athens,* XXXIV (1933–4), pp. 162–8.

and in a variety of meters they poured out reflections on their cares and joys. First came Archilochus, then a host of others; by 500 B.C. the introduction of prose had occurred.

A similar onrush occurred in the arts. Large-scale sculpture in stone and other materials had begun by 650; stone temples of the Doric order were erected in the seventh century, though more commonly thereafter. The so-called Orientalizing style in pottery, which used more supple decoration leading on to depiction of scenes from myth and epics, had emerged by 700 in Corinth, and spurred the potters of Attica to create their black-figure style before 600 B.C. (see Plate IIa). The major political events which accompanied these developments, together with the authors and thinkers who will appear in the following pages, may be found in the Chronological Table on p. 40, which will help to suggest temporal correlations.

However vigorous, the age of expansion was not one in which men automatically thought in historical terms. Lyric poets concentrated almost feverishly upon the present; in politics, art, and thought alike men fumbled half-unconsciously as they sought to formulate new patterns and institutions. In consequence this period is not one easily to be analyzed or described. Yet always the effort was to reduce the chaos of upheaval to logical forms, to find the "rhythm of life" as Archilochus put it,[3] and gradually the brilliant explorers of these two centuries, perhaps the most remarkable in all Western civilization, created a coherent view of man and the world. An unforeseen result was the evolution of concepts of space, of time, of political organization, and of human nature which could swiftly result in the appearance of the first historians soon after 500 B.C.

In this and subsequent chapters we must separate these

[3] Fr. 67a.7; see the discussion in Jaeger, *Paideia*, I, pp. 174–5. The literature of the period is discussed in Fränkel, *DuP*, chaps. iv–v; Lesky, *History of Greek Literature*, pp. 107–240; Max Treu, *Von Homer zur Lyrik* (Munich, 1955); the beginning of the era in Starr, *Origins*, pp. 221–378.

CHRONOLOGICAL TABLE

B.C.	Political Events	Literature	Philosophy/Science	Historians and Precursors
733	Crystallization of *polis* Foundation of Syracuse	Homer		
700				
650	Lelantine War	Hesiod Archilochus Callinus, Tyrtaeus, Mimnermus		
612	Second Messenian War (Fall of Nineveh)	Sappho, Alcaeus		
594	Solon as archon	Solon	Thales	
550	Tyranny of Pisistratus (Rise of Persian Empire)	Pherecydes of Syros	Anaximander, Anaximenes Pythagoras, Xenophanes	
		Anacreon, Ibycus		
500	Cleomenes of Sparta Clisthenes of Athens	Theognis Simonides	Alcmaeon Heraclitus, Parmenides	Hecataeus Acusilaus
494	Fall of Miletus			
490	Marathon			
480	Salamis			
479	Plataea			
478	Delian League	Aeschylus, Pindar	Empedocles, Anaxagoras	Pherecydes (?) Xanthus (?)
450	Leadership of Pericles	Sophocles *On Airs . . .*, *On Ancient Medicine*	Socrates, sophists	Herodotus, Hellanicus Antiochus Charon (?) Thucydides
431–404	Peloponnesian War	Euripides		

concepts and examine their crystallization and elaboration one by one. The period to be covered is that from 700 to 500, but repeatedly it will be necessary to come some distance down into the fifth century so as to gain clear examples of the result of a line of development. Of the major aspects the easiest with which to begin is the realization of space, a cardinal dimension of history, and one which has been emphasized recently by Boman as a prominent quality of the Greek outlook. Along with space as a geographical concept there emerged an awareness of the difference of peoples living within the Mediterranean world and, more specifically, of the distinct qualities of the Greeks themselves; the bearing of this ethnic distinction on the rise of history also requires consideration.

A SENSE OF SPACE

By the eighth century the Greek world was bursting its Aegean bounds, and the "way" to outward expansion lay open in the seas beyond. Odysseus wandered widely, though we cannot hope to trace his fairy-tale track; others followed more identifiable paths. The Near East, which had shaken off the effects of destruction and deterioration at the close of the Bronze Age, was now drawing together culturally and, in large measure, politically as the Assyrian Empire emerged. Greek merchants had set up a trading post at Al Mina, by the Orontes in Syria, early in the century; others made their way to Egypt, which also found Greeks useful as mercenaries, but the first established entrepôt in Egypt, Naucratis, came only late in the seventh century B.C. Contacts with the Near East were on an ever wider and more intensive scale across the age of expansion.

Here the civilized states were strong enough to limit the Greeks to their "factories." Most other shores of the Mediterranean and Black seas were inhabited by peoples who had not yet risen to the plane of civilization, and over these coasts the Greeks threw a great web of settlements, the famous Greek colonies—though in general the new settlements were independent communities.[4] In Italy and Sicily some points have recently been identified where the Greeks made temporary landfalls before 750; but the first deliberate, lasting colonies were planted after that date. Cumae is generally given the honor of having been first, about 750; the greatest Greek settlement in Sicily, Syracuse, followed in 734 or 733; and a host of other Greek colonies swiftly spread along the coasts of Greater Greece. Farther afield the Phocaeans settled Massilia in southern France in 600; the Therans colonized Cyrene on the coast of Africa in 630; other Greeks pushed down the coast of Spain, where they met and were stopped by the Carthaginians. A second wave from Greece proper and Asia Minor went north, mainly after 700, to the north coast of the Aegean, to Cyzicus in 675 and Byzantium soon thereafter, and on into the Black Sea. In this region Miletus had eventually some hundred colonies and trading posts.

The motive forces of this great outpouring lay in the social, economic, and political conditions of the eighth century B.C., an era for which our information is extremely limited. Certainly the population of Greece was increasing rapidly at this time; and most of the colonies were sited primarily as agricultural settlements, though trade was a factor of some weight. The rise of the nobility into a consciously aristocratic elite and the tensions of political life as the city-states developed also played a part in expelling men from their homeland. Archilochus was a colonist in Thasos for a time and a soldier of fortune; Alcaeus was exiled from his native Lesbos; Solon, according to tradition, left Athens for ten years after carrying out his great reforms. Most Greeks remained at home, for

[4] Starr, *Origins*, pp. 365–73; T. J. Dunbabin, *The Western Greeks* (Oxford, 1948); Carl Roebuck, *Ionian Trade and Colonization* (New York, 1959); A. J. Graham, *Colony and Mother City in Ancient Greece* (Manchester, 1964).

there were terrific dangers and labors in sailing overseas in small craft to found a colony on alien shores; yet the fluidity and restlessness in the Aegean from the eighth century onward spurred one of the most significant migrations of ancient times.

Although we cannot hope to see deeply into the motive forces for colonization, the results markedly affected the course of Greek civilization. For one, "Greece lies scattered in many regions," as a later writer put it; [5] whatever happened throughout the Mediterranean was now reflected in the previously secluded Aegean basin. The demands of the colonies for home-produced wares spurred the commerce and industry of Greece, already expanding from internal demand (especially as concentrated in the hands of the ever more luxurious aristocrats); coined money appeared as a medium of exchange and a vehicle for economic enterprise; new classes, including industrial slaves as well as merchants and artisans, began to rise in the urban centers of Athens, Corinth, Miletus, and other advanced communities. The social and economic changes were accelerated rather than damped by colonization and produced new political tensions, which at times were temporarily met by the elevation of an individual leader as "tyrant." Hellenic city-states, in other words, were forced to endure real political history, both in internal cleavages and in external clashes.

The result which concerns us most directly at this point is the growingly precise and conscious sense of space. There is no evidence that the earliest waves of colonization proceeded on any large-scale geographical plan; on the contrary, colonies came from many homelands and lay in a patchwork quilt along the coasts of Italy, Sicily, and the north Aegean. In several instances site selection was so poor as to be mocked in later tradition.[6] Gradually, nevertheless, the Greeks developed

[5] Dio Chrysostom, *Oration* 36.5.
[6] So Cyrene (Herodotus 4.156–8); Chalcedon as against Byzantium (ibid. 4.144).

a clearer knowledge of the world outside the Aegean, a knowledge which reinforced the internal tendencies of archaic civilization to visualize its physical environment more sharply. Space thus came to play a role in four quite distinct areas, those of poetry, philosophy, political organization, and geography proper.

Although poets in all eras have taken geographical license, it is difficult to feel that Homer had consciously in his mind a map of the Aegean. There are places, to be sure, in the epics, but they do not seem to lie in relation to each other within a conscious framework of space; apart from Odysseus' wanderings the poet recounts a trip of Telemachus in Greece itself (*Odyssey* 3.482ff.) which does not fit at all the real landscape of the Peloponnesus. Hesiod was almost, but not quite as vague. In the *Works and Days* he noted that in winter the sun lies farther south; or, as the poet put it in very generalized terms, that then the sun "goes to and fro over the land and city of dusky men, and shines more sluggishly upon the whole race of the Hellenes." In the *Theogony* two continents appear, Asia and Europe, but as only two among the daughters of Ocean; to the same parenthood are ascribed a variety of rivers, including Nile, Ister (Danube), Eridanus (Po), Phasis, as well as several streams of Greece and Asia Minor.[7]

As we step across the boundary of the archaic world, things change abruptly; even in the *Homeric Hymns*, cast in the old style, real geographical relationships appear. In the hymn to Delian Apollo, Leto visits the Aegean shores and islands, west, north, and south in proper order before Delos allows her to bear Apollo and Artemis on its soil; in the sequel, to Pythian Apollo, the poet recounts in specific geographical succession

[7] Hesiod, *Works and Days* 527–8; the wind comes from Thrace (507, 553), and there are references to his trip to Euboea (651ff.) and to Cyme (636). *Theogony* 337ff. (rivers), 357, 359 (Europe, Asia). Asia appears in *Iliad* 2.461 and Europe in the *Homeric Hymn to Apollo* 251, 291; but as Strabo 12.3.27 (C554) observed, Homer himself had no ideas of continents. See Thomson, *Ancient Geography*, p. 21.

the journey of Apollo to Delphi as well as his divine guidance of a ship from Cnossus around the south coast of the Peloponnesus.[8] Thereafter the lyric poets, though sparing of specific references, seem to have had a conscious realization of the relationship of places, at least in and near the Aegean. This geographical sense affected old tales as well. The adventures of Heracles were ancestral myths, but sixth-century accounts of his wanderings took him deliberately east and west, north and south, to the limits of the world visualized in that era. By the fifth century Pindar referred to the continents simply as land masses, and Herodotus could even puzzle as to why they should have been given the names of women.[9]

More coherent, if abstract, pictures of the world were hammered out by the philosophers of the sixth century, for a principal interest of the Ionian thinkers, at least as reflected in our later evidence, was cosmology. Although both divine impulses and mythical concepts still entered largely into their schemes, the basic effort of the philosophers was to create a world of logical order and physical characteristics. In the sky above, Anaximander seems not to have distinguished planets from stars, but his successor Anaximenes probably did so. Rather dubious later evidence asserts the first philosopher, Thales, observed that the Little Bear was a better guide to the pole than the Great Bear; and certainly constellations of specific names filled the firmament by this time, partly on Babylonian models. While the earth itself seems to have remained flat in philosophical thinking down well into the fifth century, Parmenides began the practice of dividing it into zones north and south. Not only was space to be visualized in systematic terms as the frame of man's life, but also this framework came to be seen as one which had changed. Xenophanes thus drew lessons from the appearance of shells inland and other phe-

[8] *Homeric Hymn*, 3.30ff., 216ff., 409ff. On Alcman's geographical interests see Bowra, *Greek Lyric Poetry*, pp. 27–8.
[9] Herodotus 4.45; Pindar, *Pyth.* 4; on Heracles, cf. Karl Schefold, *Frühgriechische Sagenbilder* (Munich, 1964), p. 66.

nomena as to the physical alteration of the world in time, a view held widely enough to appear also in Herodotus and in Xanthus, a Lydian chronicler.[1]

As philosophers ordered the world in general terms, the developing city-states found themselves forced to arrange it in very specific ways. Already by 700 B.C. the Lelantine War in Euboea had thrown Chalcis and Eretria against each other over a tiny but fertile plain; and boundaries of the *poleis* became fairly precise lines, later to be marked by forts in the case of Athens and other states. Within the individual city-state, again, space was consciously felt in the borders of land holdings, which were often delimited at Athens by the famous *horoi* or boundary stones in the days of Solon. Even more significant as an outward token of mental visualization of space is the crystallization of an urban center in the more advanced communities; at the southwest corner of the Athenian Agora, systematized from Pisistratus onward, one can still see a late sixth-century stone which proclaims "I am the border of the Agora."[2] By this date political recognition of space had proceeded so far that Clisthenes in 508/7 could reorganize the whole of Attica in new voting districts (the tribes and *trittys*) and, in doing so, calculate at least occasionally how to balance and separate local interests.[3]

[1] Thales: Callimachus fr. 191.54–5 (Pfeiffer.) Planets: Guthrie, *Greek Philosophy*, II, p. 420. Shape of earth: Guthrie, I, pp. 294–5; II, pp. 64–5, 310–11, 422. Physical change: Xenophanes fr. A 33; Strabo 1.3.4 (C49–50); Herodotus 2.12; Plato, *Critias* 111B–C, thus describes deforestation.

[2] R. E. Wycherley, *The Athenian Agora III: Literary and Epigraphical Testimonia* (Princeton, 1957), p. 218, who gives the other boundary stones which have been found. Cf. J. P. Vernant, *Les Origines de la pensée grecque* (Paris, 1962), pp. 38–9; W. A. McDonald, *The Political Meeting Places of the Greeks* (Baltimore, 1943); Roland Martin, *Recherches sur l'agora grecque* (Paris, 1951).

[3] P. Lévêque and P. Vidal-Naquet, *Clisthène l'Athénien: essai sur la représentation de l'espace et du temps dans la pensée grecque de la fin du VIᵉ siècle à la mort du Platon* (*Annales littéraires de l'université de Besançon*, LXV [Paris, 1964]), promises in its subtitle rather more than is given (but see pp. 17, 20–1); and overstates Clisthenes' calculations. See C. W. J. Eliot, *Coastal Demes of Attica*, Phoenix, Supplement V (1962).

Finally, and most obviously, the nascent sense of space manifested itself in descriptions and maps. We do not know when coastal guides, the *Periploi*, first were set down in writing, but a late source, Avienus, seems to go back to a sixth-century account of the Spanish coast. Probably the *Periegesis* by Hecataeus of Miletus was written by about 510, and the three hundred-odd fragments still extant from this work show that it was a detailed, systematic description of Mediterranean coasts and various inland districts.[4] How much Hecataeus himself had seen, beyond Egypt, is a subject for inconclusive debate; the important point is that he must have had sources of some type, even if faulty in details, for areas he had not visited. This first major geographical treatise, in prose let it be marked, was a summing-up of the Greek knowledge of the world at the close of the archaic period. Its popularity is also significant testimony to the interest of the Greeks in the space about them; though Hecataeus was scorned by Heraclitus as a simple polymath and was criticized by his successor Herodotus, his work survives in more fragments than that of any other nonpoetic thinker of the archaic period.

The first Greek map was drawn by the philosopher Anaximander, about the middle of the sixth century; but the famous map of the archaic era was also due to Hecataeus. This was probably the chart which Aristagoras of Miletus took with him on his trip to Greece to seek aid in the Ionian revolt against Persia (499–4). When the Spartans looked at it and found that the residence of the Persian king lay three months' journey inland, they ordered him out of the state in horror.[5]

By the fifth century, therefore, travel and colonization had given the Greeks a variety of information about the Mediterranean world, which they had digested into a basically factual,

[4] *Periploi:* A. Berthelot, *Festus Avienus* (Paris, 1934), pp. 108–9, 134ff.; Güngerich, *Die Küstenbeschreibung,* pp. 8–9. Hecataeus: *Hecataei Milesii Fragmenta,* ed. Giuseppe Nenci (Florence, 1954); F. Jacoby in PW *s.v.* Hekataios.
[5] Herodotus 5.49–50; Strabo 1.1.11 (C7); W. A. Heidel, *The Frame of the Ancient Greek Maps* (New York, 1937).

ordered picture of space. Soon Aeschylus could sprinkle his plays with geographical references, often precise though sometimes imaginary. When he presents Apollo as warning Orestes that the Furies "will pursue you over the wide continent, beyond the sea and sea-girt cities, over the traveled earth," the phrase is, while general in nature, far more geographically conscious than any Homer would have written. By the last decades of the fifth century common Athenians were able to draw each other maps of the fateful way to Syracuse.[6]

In this knowledge there were many blunders, as in Herodotus' geographical descriptions; for measures of distance and direction were necessarily primitive. Ideas of space, in truth, did not really enter intimately into men's thinking. In the sculpture and vases of the period terrain was suggested, if at all, in the most limited fashion; [7] and the world beyond the nearest hills was one of imagination for the ordinary Greek, who traveled little. Even leaders such as Pindar and Herodotus visualized the regions outside the known world as filled with exotic peoples. Beyond the Pillars of Heracles, Pindar proclaimed, one could not sail, though Greek mariners certainly had actually done so on occasion.[8]

The writing of history, however, was to concern itself with the Mediterranean world, and within this area space had now become a conscious intellectual element. It could be described, could be mapped, and could even be analyzed as to

[6] Plutarch, *Nicias* 12; Aeschylus, *Eumenides* 75-7. See also Aeschylus, *Agamemnon* 281ff.; *Persians* 16ff., 232, 864; *Suppliants* 255ff., 547ff. But the wanderings of Io (*Prometheus Bound* 707-35), while methodical, are imaginary.

[7] Terrain indications become extensive only from about 400 B.C. on. Cf. *CVA* Austria 1, pl. 42 (Wien 1), Inv. 382, a skyphos of 400 B.C. or later, where Antiope climbs in rocky terrain; earlier examples, with a rock, column, or the like, may be found in *CVA* Denmark 3, pl. 145 (Copenhagen 3), Inv. 6327; *CVA* Italy 25, pl. 1156 (Tarquinia 1), RC 6846, by Brygos; *CVA* Italy 20, pl. 990 (Naples 1), Inv. 81159, 500-490 B.C.; and others. The problems of perspective and of efforts to suggest distance do not enter into this early period to any significant extent.

[8] Pindar, *Nem.* 4.69-70. Idealization of peoples beyond the known world appears in Aeschylus, *Prometheus Unbound*, fr. 196, and thereafter.

its varying effects on the men who lived within it. Some of this analysis occurs in Herodotus; the most extended and scientific consideration of the topic in the fifth century is the Hippocratic monograph *On Airs Waters Places,* which very directly concerns itself with the results of geography and climate for the flora, fauna, and human societies of cold Scythia, hot Egypt, and moderate clime of Greece itself.[9]

GREEKS AND BARBARIANS

Although space is a major dimension of history, it is only in very recent times that physical geography has become an independent discipline; the ancient Greeks almost never visualized their Mediterranean world apart from the peoples who inhabited its terrain. A passionate curiosity about mankind stamped Hellenic culture and eventually gave rise to those clear, if exaggerated, views about the diversity of human societies which are revealed in the treatise *On Airs Waters Places* and also in the history of Herodotus. Ethnographic awareness lay in the background of historical thinking, particularly in respect to the antithesis Greek–barbarian.

Homer knew of non-Achaean peoples, many of which he listed in the catalogue of Trojan allies. Some of these he even called "barbarian," i.e., non-Greek speaking, for the term initially meant only those who uttered "bar-bar" rather than Greek dialects. But culturally Homer seems to have drawn no sharp lines; Trojans and Achaeans acted and lived in much the same manner and talked to each other as equals without any need for interpreters. At this point, evidently, the Greeks scarcely knew an outside world.

[9] *Hippocrates,* tr. W. H. S. Jones, I (London, 1923). Felix Heinimann, *Nomos und Physis* (Basel, 1945), pp. 13ff., considers the treatise independent of Herodotus and dates it just before the Peloponnesian War (p. 209). The idea later was a commonplace, as in Aristotle, *Politics* 7.6.1 (1327b.29ff.).

When Greek colonists and travelers went abroad in numbers, the sense of difference necessarily became sharper. Aristeas seems to have visited south Russia in the seventh century and helped to set later views of the exotic Issedones and Arimaspes; Archilochus lived on the border between Greek culture and Thracian barbarism.[1] If we ourselves could see these two worlds, we might feel inclined to consider them almost on the same plane of civilization, but to Archilochus there was certainly a distinction between Hellene and non-Hellene.

Far more important a cultural frontier was the Near East; and our information suggests that aristocratic, more consciously perceptive Greek travelers went mainly in this direction, for a variety of purposes. These men saw the impressive evidences of past Pharaonic and Babylonian achievements as well as the developed civilization of the Assyrian period. Greek mercenaries made their way up the Nile to Abu Simbel about 594–89 and there carved on the knee of a statue of Ramses II their names. Sappho's brother traded to Egypt and to Sappho's displeasure fell into the hands of an Egyptian courtesan; Alcaeus' brother served in Babylon before the close of the seventh century.[2] Alcaeus himself spoke of the Nile from his own knowledge; so too did Solon, Hecataeus, and eventually Herodotus.

Especially after the rise of the Persian Empire, which held subject the Greeks of Cyprus, Cilicia, the coast of Asia Minor, and even the north coast of the Aegean, Greeks traveled voluntarily inland to Mesopotamia and Persia. Darius em-

---

[1] J. D. P. Bolton, *Aristeas of Proconnesus* (Oxford, 1962); on Archilochus, Fränkel, *DuP*, p. 167. See generally Julius Jüthner, *Hellenen und Barbaren* (Leipzig, 1923); Hans Schwabl and co-authors, *Entretiens Hardt VIII: Grecs et Barbares* (Geneva, 1961); H. C. Baldry, *The Unity of Mankind in Greek Thought* (Cambridge, 1965); Karl Trüdinger, *Studien zur Geschichte der griechisch-römischen Ethnographie* (Basel, 1918).

[2] Tod, *GHI*, I, no. 4; Alcaeus 350 LP; Sappho 5 and 15 LP; later Plato, *Republic* 9.579B–C, could speak of travel as a natural activity of a "free man."

ployed a Greek seaman, Scylax of Caryanda, to explore India; Greek artists worked at Persepolis; and Democedes from far-off Croton in Italy served as royal physician at the Persian court.[3] Among the refugees from the internecine strife of the Greek states was that former king of Sparta, Demaratus, in whose mouth Herodotus places some of his most significant comparisons between Greek and Persian ways.

The results of this awareness of the outside world were twofold. On the one hand the Greeks became more conscious of their own nature, as distinct and also—in their eyes—as greatly superior to "barbarian" ways; and on the other they exhibited a fairly objective interest in how alien peoples lived. The latter, which we may consider first, can be found in a wide range of contemporary evidence.

In pottery, for example, a north Ionian vase from Smyrna, of about 540/30 B.C., depicts a Bactrian camel led by a man in homespuns, an un-Hellenic dress.[4] Archers in Scythian garb appear on Attic vases from the middle of the sixth century (see Plate Va), though it remains debatable whether they are always intended to be actual Scythians; the earliest examples may even be drawn from the wild Cimmerians of the seventh century, who ravaged Asia Minor.[5] An exotic framework is

[3] Herodotus 4.44; H. Bengtson, "Skylax von Karyanda und Herakleides von Mylasa," *Historia*, III (1954), pp. 301–7; Paul Fabre, "La date de la rédaction du périple de Scylax," *Etudes classiques*, XXXIII (1965), pp. 353–66, places the *periplus* under his name about 361–57 B.C. Democedes: Herodotus 3.125, 129–37. Artists: G. M. A. Richter, "Greeks in Persia," *American Journal of Archaeology*, L (1946), pp. 15–30, quoting the building inscriptions of Susa; Carl Nylander, "The Toothed Chisel in Pasargadae," ibid., LXX (1966), pp. 373–6, promises more extensive studies.

[4] J. M. Cook, *Annual of the British School at Athens*, LX (1965), pp. 123–4, pl. 30.

[5] C. H. Emilie Haspels, *Attic Black-figured Lekythoi* (Paris, 1936), p. 38, with bibliography; G. M. A. Richter, *CVA USA* 11 (Metropolitan Museum 2), p. 15, on 25.78.6 (pl. 24); Helmut Schoppa, *Die Darstellung der Perser in der griechischen Kunst bis zum Beginn des Hellenismus* (Coburg, 1933), pp. 10–11. On the François vase, by Klitias about 570 B.C., an archer is named *Kimmerios:* P. E. Arias and M. Hirmer, *Tausend Jahre griechische Vasenkunst* (Munich, 1960), pl. 42.

clearly suggested on the Arcesilaus cup of Cyrene (Plate III) as well as in the shaven priests of the Busiris vase (Plate VIIb); in the purely Attic scene of mourning shown on Plate VI the nurse at the head of the bier has Thracian tattoo marks. Greek art, nonetheless, remained so specifically Hellenic in content that even Persians are rare on Attic red-figured vases of the fifth century (see Plate Vb). To a considerable extent the struggles between Persians and Greeks seem to have been transmuted into Amazonomachias, Centauromachias, or battles of the Giants.[6]

Authors of the archaic and classic eras went further in illustrating an awareness of difference between Greeks and barbarians. Anaximander, though often presented as a purely theoretical cosmologist, had an interest in the actual world, both geographically and anthropologically.[7] The greatest exponent of the practical side in Ionian thought down to 500 was Hecataeus, who provided a variety of anthropological information in his *Periegesis*. Even more illustrative is the testimony of the plays of Aeschylus, which suggest that his audience enjoyed a foreign flavor; two of the surviving seven Aeschylean tragedies are laid abroad, and a third involves mainly Egyptian women.[8]

---

[6] Schoppa, *Die Darstellung der Perser*, pp. 51–4, observes that barbarian costumes on vases are generally a "Phantasieprodukt"; Anne Bovon, "La Représentation des guerriers perses et la notion de barbare dans la l^{re} moitié du Ve siècle," *Bulletin de correspondance hellénique*, LXXXVII (1963), pp. 579–602, gives fifteen examples in the period. Cf. J. Boardman, *Greek Art* (New York, 1964), p. 186; Dietrich von Bothmer, *Amazons in Greek Art* (Oxford, 1957); Francis Vian, *La Guerre des géants* (Paris, 1952).

Negroes, it may be noted, appear mostly from the fifth century on; cf. Haspels, *Attic Black-figured Lekythoi*, pp. 103–4, and Grace H. Beardsley, *The Negro in Greek and Roman Civilization* (Baltimore, 1929).

[7] W. A. Heidel, "Anaximander's Book, The Earliest Known Geographical Treatise," *Proceedings of the American Academy of Arts and Sciences*, LVI (1921), pp. 237–88; Guthrie, *Greek Philosophy*, I, p. 75.

[8] Distinctions between Greeks and foreigners are drawn by Aeschylus in *Agamemnon* 109, 578, 919, 1254; *Persians* 85–6, 182–3; *Suppliants* 201, 234, 497, 761; cf. Baldry, *Unity of Mankind*, pp. 16–18, and p. 55, n. 4, below.

Without seeking to survey all the evidence given by Herodotus, whose charm lies partly in his detailed description of alien folkways, one can never overlook that fascinating passage in which he observes that each person, given the opportunity to choose "the set of beliefs which he thought best," would inevitably choose those of his own country. To prove the point he recounts the experiment of Darius, who assembled the Greeks at his court and asked how much money they would take to eat the corpses of their fathers. When they rejected the idea in horror, he called in some Indians, who did follow this custom, and inquired what reward they would require to burn the dead. "The Indians exclaimed aloud, and bade him forbear such language. Such is men's custom; and Pindar was right, in my judgment, when he said, 'Law is king over all.' " [9] The attitude which Herodotus conveys in graphic detail was later, among the sophists, to lead to an ever wider and more theoretical consideration of *nomos* as "law" or "convention."

The objectivity of Herodotus' tale also helps to explain why later ancient critics could criticize him as favoring the barbarians; but the charge has as little substance for the Father of History as for his countrymen in general. When the Greeks came to know the barbarians, they calmly and certainly considered themselves and their customs superior and so took Hellas as the yardstick for measurement.

Hesiod already had in mind a concept of the Hellene as a distinct entity and tried in the *Theogony* to explain its origin; Archilochus first used the term "panhellene," which thereafter summed up the many varied peoples of Greece. Toward the close of the sixth century the philosopher Xenophanes thus praised a person as "a man whose fame shall reach all over Hellas, and shall not cease so long as the race of Hellenic bards exists." Perhaps the most magnificent definition of what the term Hellas came to mean is afforded during the Athenian

[9] Herodotus 3.38; Pindar fr. 169S-187T. Cf. Pindar fr. 215S-188T, which asserts that customs vary according to men and that each praises his own usages.

refusal to make terms with Persia after Salamis; to the Spartans they explained,

> There is our common brotherhood with the Greeks: our common language, the altars and sacrifices of which we all partake, the common character which we bear—did the Athenians betray all these, of a truth it would not be well.[1]

The sense of superiority pervading this passage is typical of the opposition between Greek and non-Greek. In visiting hoary Egypt the Greeks could admit that their own civilization was far younger and were willing to seek tokens of indebtedness; those who visited Assyrian or Persian courts knew that, in contrast, poverty was one's neighbor in Greece. Nonetheless their own pride in the burgeoning Aegean world left in them no sense of cultural insecurity or inferiority; even politically a Greek poet proclaimed, "The law-abiding *polis,* though small and set on a lofty rock, outranks senseless Nineveh." [2] So Herodotus traveled widely abroad, appreciated foreign cultures so far that he could even suggest that much of life was merely a matter of custom, and yet remained sure in his mind that the Hellenic way was best.

While the Hellenic outlook and standards of values were expressed in a mass of gnomic poetry, the sense of superiority was summed up in the evolution of the term *barbaros* to mean not simply "alien-speaking" but also "inferior." This shift probably took place across the archaic period, though the available evidence suggests that Baldry is right in arguing that the Persian Wars "gave the antithesis its emotional force." [3] In Aeschylus' *Persians,* performed in 472 B.C., the Greeks are

[1] Herodotus 8.144.2; Xenophanes fr. 6; Hesiod fr. 7 (Rzach). On the concept of Hellas, see Heuss, *Antike und Abendland,* II (1946), pp. 29–35; and note also the role of the *Hellanodikai* in the Olympic games from the beginning from the sixth century (a specific example of their activity is given in Herodotus 5.22).

[2] Phocylides fr. 4.

[3] Baldry, *Unity of Mankind,* p. 22; cf. Hans Diller, *Entretiens Hardt,* VIII, pp. 39ff.

proclaimed "slaves to no lord," a theme steadily evolved thereafter in Hellenic thought to separate Greeks as naturally free
and barbarians as equally naturally slaves. The kindred idea
that barbarians lived on a lower cultural and intellectual level
appears in Herodotus' observation that "the Greeks have been
from very ancient times distinguished from the barbarians by
superior sagacity and freedom from foolish simpleness." [4]
Thereafter the distinction appeared more bluntly in Euripides
and Thucydides, and became a commonplace in fourth-
century writers such as Xenophon, Isocrates, and Aristotle.[5] In
more extreme theoretical statements this concept drew close to
equaling modern racial theories, but practice fortunately
never came in close correlation with theory. Greeks could live
with barbarians and appreciate their qualities while yet re-
taining their Hellenic spirit; Greek historians, though patriotic, were able to appreciate non-Greek achievements. To this
latter quality the great celebrations of Rome by Polybius and
Dionysius of Halicarnassus bear ample witness.

The Greeks were not the only people in history to feel
themselves superior and set apart when they came repeatedly
in contact with outlanders; but the extraordinarily rational
and analytical quality of Greek civilization, as it had developed by the close of the age of expansion, drove them on to
assess and describe the differences and to explain why these
existed. This effort led to an exploration of the effects of
geography and climate, as in the Hippocratic treatise already

[4] Herodotus 1.60; Aeschylus, *Persians* 241–2, cf. *Suppliants* 760f., 962f.
Observe also in Aeschylus, *Suppliants* 220 and *Seven* 269, the phrases for
"Greek customs"; in the former play the king of Argos tells the Egyptian
herald (914), "For a barbarian that has to do with Hellenes, you wax
overproud."
[5] So Sophocles, *Ajax* 1259–63; Euripides, *Iphigenia in Aulis* 1400–1;
Thucydides 1.6.5; Xenophon, *Anabasis* 5.4.34; Aristotle, *Politics* 1.1.5
(1252b.6–7) and 1.2.19 (1255a.33–5); other examples in Baldry, *Unity
of Mankind*, pp. 62–72. Cf. Helen H. Bacon, *Barbarians in Greek
Tragedy* (New Haven, 1961). Yet the fifth century already knew the
concept of mankind as a single race: Euripides, *Alexander* fr. 52;
Sophocles, *Tereus* fr. 532; and the sophists (Baldry, *Unity of Mankind*,
pp. 37, 43–4).

noted; but the great monument of this approach was the history of Herodotus. In his first five books Herodotus surveyed the ways of life and previous development of a great arc of peoples from Scythia to Libya; then in the last four came the pitting of this Near Eastern world against indomitable Hellas. Only after the Greeks had developed a geographical sense of space could he have composed such a widely sweeping yet ordered treatment; but the emotional, even spiritual tone of his history incarnated the kindred development of an awareness of the unique qualities summed up in the word Hellas.

CHAPTER 3

THE FRAMEWORK

OF TIME

For a modern historian the concept of time appears to be an objective, if fundamental, quality of human affairs, marked off quite simply by mechanical celestial phenomena. When historians do fall into conscious argument about temporal matters, it is always over the assignment of a precise date to a specific event; historical narratives themselves proceed methodically from the past to the present. Our present chronological system of solar years numbered back and forward from the birth of Jesus and subdivided into schematic months was evolved only in the sixth century after Christ but has become so instinctive that anthropologists seek to extend it via carbon-14 measurement and other devices into prehistoric eras.

If this is all that the word "time" means, then we shall have trouble finding it in ancient Greek thought; or, alternatively, we may well be misled into emphasizing the wrong aspects of Greek temporal speculation. This is not an idle remark, for many students of historiography have been thus misdirected. As a preliminary step let me essay to clear away some common misconceptions before we investigate those archaic developments which did produce a historical framework of time alongside that of space.

The Greeks never agreed upon a universally accepted yard-

57

stick of time, for the system of dating by Olympiads was an artificial, late construction. Rather, each city-state had a list of eponymous officials, such as that of the archons at Athens, and might well subdivide its year in a distinctive fashion. When Herodotus arrived on the scene, he could only seek to establish relative correlations between these individual chronological schemes, insofar as he made any effort to "date" events; but so cavalier was the first historian in this respect that some recent students of historiography have accused him of lacking a real sense of time. To make matters worse Herodotus, like the poets, occasionally turned matters upside down by moving from the present into the past.

Yet certainly the work of Herodotus was historical in the sense that time, as well as space, was a cardinal dimension of his narrative. One great achievement of archaic Greece was the visualization of the human present as a concrete stage as against other stages in the past, but organically connected with that past in the flow of time. This concept, which pervades Herodotus' history, is the fundamental base of historical time, though nowadays it is heavily overladen by an emphasis on chronology proper. In view of modern theories of evolution it may also be desirable to observe that the connection of past and present was not conceived often in ancient Greece as a process of *continuous* alteration.

Even so, time came to be considered in some circles as bringing change. Such a historical interpretation was not easily developed. Still today time becomes an abstract, almost mysterious entity once we move beyond a purely chronological framework; St. Augustine well said, "What is time then? If nobody asks me, I know; but if I were desirous to explain it to one that should ask me, plainly I know not." [1] Nor are time and space as distinct as logical analysis might suggest; space may be measured in terms of the time which a journey, for

[1] Augustine, *Confessions* 11.14 (tr. W. Watts).

instance, will take, and time has often been visualized in a spatial manner, as a line or circle.

Particularly in archaic Greece, which looked at its world through the spectacles of epic and myth and was still organized in a very primitive social and religious structure, the emergence of a sense of historical time could only be gradual and incomplete. The thinkers and poets of the archaic era, bred in conservative traditions, faced terrific intellectual and social problems in the age of upheaval and expansion; the marvel is that they proceeded so far toward an orderly acceptance of time as change rather than rejecting the idea utterly on the one hand or yielding to pure ephemerism on the other.

Not only must we think of time in broader terms than the purely chronological if we are to identify the vital clues to its presence in early Greek literature and art; but also—and above all—we cannot read the philosophers such as Plato and Aristotle, who talked directly of time, and then assume that these philosophical treatments represented the approach of contemporary historians. This error is nonetheless fallacious for being ubiquitous. Philosophers and historians in any age may share many of the same preconceptions and fundamental attitudes, but it is not often easy to prove that either discipline has consciously affected the views of the other. Philosophers rarely draw their materials for thought from history, and historians are not often philosophical by temperament; the philosopher, the mathematician, and the astronomer of today talk of time in quite different terms from those of the historian.[2]

[2] M. Heidegger, "Der Zeitbegriff in der Geschichtswissenschaft," *Zeitschrift für Philosophie und philosophische Kritik*, CLXI (1916), pp. 171–88, and *Sein und Zeit* (6th ed.; Tübingen, 1949), pp. 428–33; Henri Bergson, *Essai sur les données immédiates de la conscience* (7th ed.; Paris, 1909), chap. ii. I have dealt with some confusions in the matter in "Historical and Philosophical Time," *History and Theory*, Beiheft VI (1966), pp. 24–35; see also the preceding essay in the Beiheft by A. Momigliano, "Time in Ancient Historiography."

In ancient Greek philosophy and history the visible differences in planes of inquiry and methods of approach stand as warning against any conflation of the two disciplines. Whereas history dealt with specific and temporal events in human society, philosophy settled eventually upon a search for the eternally true, quite often on a divine, abstract plane. In this respect it linked onto religious concepts; as far as time itself was concerned, philosophic views were largely derived from astronomical speculation.[3] The result was that Greek philosophic time was frequently, though not always, cast in cyclical terms.

This theoretical line of approach must be kept in mind as we proceed, for it arose out of one significant side of early Greek thought. Yet archaic civilization was possessed of many, often contradictory drives, and these philosophic discussions which postulated an unchanging substratum or spoke of life in cycles did not necessarily or fully represent the kind of time that a man of the era had in mind as he recounted earthly events. When history finally appeared, its recital was not to be framed in cyclical terms.

To follow, then, the slow awakening of a historically oriented consciousness of time we must go back before philosophy itself had developed, and investigate the evidence of archaic poetry and art, as well as of the Greek language itself. Although this material adequately shows the reluctance of early Hellas to yield a sense of timeless continuity, the Greeks had come by 500 B.C. to a view of time in human affairs which made history possible, even essential, as a mode by which society explained its present character through the action of time in the past.

[3] P. Vidal-Naquet, "Temps des dieux et temps des hommes," *Revue de l'histoire des religions*, CLVII (1960), pp. 55–80; Victor Goldschmidt, *Le Système stoïcien et l'idée de temps* (Paris, 1953), pp. 50–4, and the essays by Fränkel and Accame cited above, p. 16, n. 4.

CONTINUITY AND CONSERVATISM

Since the nineteenth century the sense of irresistible change
has become an imperious despot in Western society. Marxist
hopes rest upon its inevitability; capitalistic thinkers can even
argue, if mistakenly, that the past has no value as a guide for
our headlong rush into the future. This awareness of time as
change is in reality a relatively new conquest in the Western
world, one which furnishes a very poor base for proper comprehension of ancient Greek society. Hellenic culture was
always "in the grip of the past," as a recent work so entitled
demonstrates for every field of activity.[4]

Down to at least 700 B.C. an intuitive feeling of unchanging
continuity exercised its unconscious domination. Even in the
more developed civilizations of the Near East the weight lay
heavily on the side of conservatism, which required the reten-
tion of patterns long ago given to man by Marduk and Ishtar
or by Osiris and Ptah. In Greece too the gods of Mount
Olympus, as well as less sharply defined forces, were felt to
have established the ways of mankind as recounted in the
myths, "the agents of stability." Across the Dark Ages the rude
simplicity of economic, social, and political organization en-
hanced the power of the traditional mold; quite probably any
change or unexpected upheaval, by threatening the patterns
which supported this simple life, was considered a social
danger rather than an asset. "The ancient custom," said Hesiod, "is the best." [5]

[4] B. A. van Groningen, *In the Grip of the Past* (Leiden, 1953); Selincourt, *World of Herodotus*, pp. 120–1. On modern time see, among many
works, S. G. F. Brandon, *Time and Mankind: An Historical and Philosophical Study of Mankind's Attitude to the Phenomena of Change*
(London, 1951); Lewis Einstein, *Historical Change* (Cambridge, 1946);
Hans Meyerhoff, *Time in Literature* (Berkeley, 1955); Stephen Toulmin
and June Goodfield, *The Discovery of Time* (New York, 1965).
[5] Hesiod fr. 221 (Rzach), of sacrifices; Aristotle, *Metaphysics* 1.3.6

The inherited lack of a sharp temporal sense is particularly manifest in the Greek verb, the forms of which had only limited temporal connotation. The present tense may express some state universally valid, in the past as well as in the future; the aorist tense can be employed for general certainties and lasting truths. Yet alongside these timeless states it deserves to be noticed that rudimentary temporal distinctions did exist. The imperfect form might be used to affirm a duration in the past, and the perfect group of tenses could suggest that an event in the past was not dead, but in part determined the present. One line of Homer's *Iliad* (1.70) thus distinguishes clearly "things that were, and that were to be, and that had been before." [6]

In general, however, the Greeks came to the age of expansion without any conscious realization of temporal differences; the available evidence, artistic as well as literary, suggests rather the maintenance of ancestral patterns, which changed in Geometric pottery only slowly. As a psychologist has thoughtfully commented with regard to the emergence of the historical sense, human societies must experience at length and on a large scale changes in their mode of life before they can visualize that their past is different from their present. [7]

By the fifth century much had changed in the Greek world, but the spirit of continuity remained strong. So marked in our eyes, indeed, are the alterations in Greek civilization following the great outburst about 700 B.C. that we are all too likely to

---

(983b.32), could still observe, "What is most ancient is most revered." The earlier quotation above comes from Frank Kermode, *The Sense of an Ending* (New York, 1967), p. 39.

[6] Verb: van Groningen, *In the Grip of the Past,* pp. 22–3; Jean Humbert, *Syntaxe grecque* (2d ed.; Paris, 1954), p. 137 #232. Homer means only that Calchas knows all things of all eras (Snell, *Varia Variorum,* p. 9); but in Hesiod, *Theogony* 37–8, the phrase implies *continuity.* Cf. fr. 68 of the *Catalogue-Eoiae* (Berlin papyrus 10560) and G. S. Kirk, *Heraclitus: The Cosmic Fragments* (Cambridge, 1954), p. 310, for other examples.

[7] I. Meyerson, "Le temps, la mémoire, l'histoire," *Journal de psychologie,* LIII (1956), pp. 333–54, at p. 336; see also Fraisse, *Psychologie du temps,* pp. 151ff.

minimize its strongly conservative quality. Most men still lived in the fifth century in a simple farming pattern; superstition and magic, as well as religious ritual, held a grip which was somewhat hidden in classic authors but was nonetheless strong; despite the great development of art and literature, the effort was always to create forms or molds in which to contain and express the new ways of thought. So the temple plan, well established by 700, was ever elaborated as the prime architectural form; and vases of the sixth and fifth centuries (e.g., Plates IIa, IV, VI) continued earlier shapes or systems of decoration despite their ever more skillful techniques.

This grip of the past often evolved into conscious conservatism. The poetry of Theognis, late in the sixth century, was one long complaint against social disturbance, coupled with praise of ancestral aristocratic ways; together with other poetry of the same type the elegiacs of Theognis were so popular in the fifth century that, alone of all poets in the age of expansion, his work survived entire. Before the end of the century the oligarchic revolution of 411 B.C. in Athens was deliberately to seek the restoration of "an ancestral constitution"; at Sparta, we are told, nothing was heard as readily as tales of the past.[8] This conservatism stretched so far that people looked back with nostalgia to earlier ways of dress, while historical inscriptions were recut to secure their survival.

On a more abstract level the main avenue of philosophic advance was to elaborate a pattern of the world which was static in fundamental principles. Philosophers found it almost inconceivable that something might come from nothing, that new things emerged;[9] from Parmenides' theory of an eternally

---

[8] Theognis 39ff., 283ff., 615ff., 635ff., 647ff., etc.; Plato, *Hippias Major* 285D.

[9] Mario Untersteiner, *Senofane: testimonianze e frammenti* (Florence, 1956), pp. xxxix, cvii–ix; Aristotle, *Metaphysics* 11.6.4 (1062b.24–26); Parmenides fr. 8, "And it never Was nor Will Be, because it Is Now." The word *chronos*, parenthetically, does not appear in the extant fragments of Parmenides.

changeless universe the road led on straight to the majestic constructions of Plato's idealistic system. By the fifth century this wing of Greek thought expressed an essentially deliberate posture, one which thereby manifested awareness of change. Even Parmenides distinguished between the abstract world of Truth and the mortal, delusionary world of *doxai*, "appearances," which altered; in the contemporary speculation of men like Heraclitus and later Empedocles change played a significant role, though often on a cyclical path; Xenophanes had concluded from the finding of shells and fossils in rocks that once the sea covered the land.[1]

Theoretically this strongly conservative attitude might have led thinking men to look at the past in order to correct the mistakes of the present. Occasionally traces of this procedure may be found, as has just been noted; but on the whole the traditional emphasis in Greek civilization on continuity hampered, rather than favored, the emergence of history alongside myth and abstract speculation.

THE AWARENESS OF TIME

The fundamental force which eventually impelled men to visualize time as change was the great upheaval during the age of expansion. After 700 B.C. the Greeks were thrown abroad over many shores of the Mediterranean; at home they experienced tremendous alterations in political and social organization, as well as in arts and letters. Clear awareness of these changes and meditation on their effects on human society, however, was a slow development, not all aspects of which are well lit in our surviving literary evidence. What

[1] See above, p. 46, n. 1, Heraclitus frr. 60, 103 (Guthrie, *Greek Philosophy*, I, pp. 452, 465–68, 487); Mario Untersteiner, *Parmenide: testimonianze e frammenti* (Florence, 1958), pp. clxvi–ccx; Guthrie, *Greek Philosophy*, II, pp. 167ff., 247–55 on Empedocles.

does remain suggests a remarkable oscillation between fascination in the past and absorption in the fleeting present; only in the sixth century did past and present come into a conscious, orderly connection.

Although Homer sensed that the past was different from the present, the present was not a matter for his immediate comment. Nor was the epic past described in chronological terms. The aged Nestor might spin tales of preceding generations, and the sun rose and set over the plain of Troy; but time and space in epic and myth alike were illusionary qualities of a world far removed from human reality. So too in Hesiod's *Theogony* the origins of the world and of the gods unfolded in a logical sequence unconnected with human time.

In Hesiod's *Works and Days*, on the other hand, a scheme of sharply distinguished races covered the development of mankind down into the poet's own time, the age of iron. A promising beginning, we might think, for really historical speculation, but unfortunately the lyric and elegiac poets of the seventh century turned sharply away from the past. As these poets looked about their world, they saw first its changeableness. The word *ephemeros*, "of the day," symbolizes their views; the color of men, proclaimed Archilochus, is the color of the days which Zeus brings, and their thoughts are those of the actions in which they engage. Stumbling into a sense of human personality, poets poured out their loves and hates of the moment and fiercely reveled in the present, for "as soon as a man is dead, he is no longer respected by his fellow-citizens." [2] So spoke Archilochus in the mid-seventh century; to attest the enduring strength of this point of view Simonides of Ceos, in the early fifth, struck the same note.

[2] Archilochus frr. 64–5, 68; Simonides frr. 8, 48, 59. In Archilochus *chronos* appears only in fr. 91 (Lasserre, restored) and fr. 250 (Lasserre, not certainly Archilochean); references to the past are far more numerous and to the future (as frr. 1, 44). See in general Fränkel, *DuP*, pp. 148–50, and "Man's 'Ephemeros' Nature according to Pindar and Others," *Transactions of the American Philological Association,* LXXVII (1946), pp. 131–45.

In pottery the break from the rigid conventions of the Geometric style to the exuberant, swirling designs of the Orientalizing period was as sharp, and led at times, especially in the Protoattic work of the seventh century, to decorations which lost almost all sense of order. Change became so rapid and so conscious that modern students can seek to date vases to a specific decade. Yet the ceramic developments illustrate a vital aspect of time in archaic Greece, for the potters never quite surrendered their ties to the past in the joy of creation in the present. Some workshops conservatively clung to Geometric attitudes long after others had moved forward; even these latter artists did not abandon their inherited sense of disciplined form. By the mid-sixth century, when Exekias created his marvelous scene of Dionysus sailing across the sea (Plate IIa), Attic potters had won their way through the epoch of upheaval and were advancing in a sure manner. Particularly in these Attic workshops, but also to a lesser degree at Corinth and elsewhere, a favorite source of illustration was the legendary past of epic and myth, clearly identified by the addition of written names beside the characters depicted; but alongside the figures of epic on the vases a host of handsome young Attic nobles parade on horseback or engage in athletics in the present.

By this time poets had come to link the present, as a consciously felt point of time, with the future and also with the real past, which they distinguished at least partially from the world of epic. Even in the seventh century Mimnermus of Colophon sang of the coming of the Greek settlers to Asia, and Tyrtaeus linked the earlier Spartan conquest of Messenia two generations before his time to the revolt of the Messenians which led to his own battle songs. In the same period the poet Callinus specifically emphasized the invasion of the wild Cimmerians "now." [3]

The decisive evidence for a clear temporal sense is that

[3] Mimnermus frr. 10, 12; Tyrtaeus in Strabo 8.4.10 (C 362); his fr. 4 gives the Second Messenian War as lasting twenty years; Callinus fr. 3.

provided by the elegies of Solon, just on either side of 600 B.C. Solon, an Athenian aristocrat who traveled commercially in the eastern Mediterranean, is also the first political figure to stand out as a real personality in Greek history. He rose to fame at Athens through his exhortations to his fellow citizens to regain the offshore island of Salamis, then held by the Megarians; in these patriotic elegies his deep interest in present concerns is manifest. Thereafter his attention, and his poetry, shifted to the social and economic oppression which poor agricultural debtors were experiencing at the hands of the aristocrats. In 594 the community elected Solon "archon and reconciler" in an effort to deal with their problems without open revolution.

The surviving bits and pieces of Solon's elegies are more firmly set in a framework of real time than is any other poetry down to 500 B.C. Solon was involved actively in the present, but he considered the social ills of his day as a change from the past; in one line he mourned how Athens, as the oldest land of Ionia, was being slain by its contentions. Even more, he visualized time as running on into the future and was unusually confident as to the results it would bring. Mimnermus' strong presentism had led him to grieve over the ills of old age; Solon firmly disagreed in a famous passage, with which may be coupled his comment, "As I grow old I learn many things." [4] Twice he appealed to the verdict of time on his reforms: Mother Earth would stand witness for his liberation of its soil from mortgages and its farms from debt "in the judgment of time"; or again, "the truth will out, and a little time will show my fellow-citizens, sure enough, whether I be mad or no." [5] This latter statement is the first surviving example of the employment of *chronos* as subject of a sentence.

In both passages there is a hint of the idea that time is a self-moving force in human affairs. Soon thereafter this view

---

[4] Frr. 4 and 22; cf. his analysis of life as falling in seven-year periods in fr. 19.
[5] Fr. 24, line 3; fr. 9. Cf. fr. 3, line 16, and fr. 1.

became prominent and remained significant in Greek thought. The earliest extant philosophical fragment, from Anaximander about 550 B.C., thus affirms that "things give justice and make reparation to one another for their injustice, according to the arrangement of Time (κατὰ τὴν τοῦ χρόνου τάξιν)," a phrase strikingly similar to Solon's "judgment of time." [6] Pherecydes of Syros made time one of the fundamental principles in his esoteric cosmogony, in the sense of a force for change; this theory recurred in later Orphic thought, though verbal confusions between Chronos and the father of Zeus, Kronos, must be kept in mind in assessing its meaning.[7] More significant in the present connection was the continuing celebration across the fifth century of time itself as a divine force of change, to which man was subject.

In deifying time the Greeks perhaps sought to exorcise its potentialities for bringing change in human society; and in such celebrations as the chant of Sophocles' chorus in the *Electra*, "Time is a god who makes rough ways smooth," we seem to be far removed from a historical concept of time.[8] In this respect it is notable that Solon's own references to *chronos* would seem to imply that he visualized it less as an active, independent force than as a quantitative measure—the rich plastic sense of the Greeks often makes it difficult to distin-

---

[6] Anaximander fr. 1, a much debated fragment. See G. S. Kirk and J. E. Raven, *The Presocratic Philosophers* (Cambridge, 1957), p. 120; Accame, *Rivista di filologia*, n.s. XXXIX (1961), p. 382 n. 2; Jaeger, *Paideia*, I, pp. 217–19; Charles H. Kahn, *Anaximander and the Origin of Greek Cosmology* (New York, 1960), pp. 166ff.; G. Vlastos, *Philosophical Quarterly*, II (1952), p. 108, who takes the concept as only a metaphor (erroneously, I think).

[7] Kirk and Raven, *Presocratic Philosophers*, pp. 48–57; Antonio Battegazzore and Mario Untersteiner, *Sofisti: testimonianze e frammenti*, IV (Florence, 1962), pp. 294–5; on the very doubtful efforts to connect these views with Persian ideas of Zervan Akarana see Enzo Degani, ΑΙΩΝ *da Omero ad Aristotele* (Padua, 1961), pp. 107–16, with good bibliography.

[8] *Electra* 179 (tr. Jebb); cf. Sophocles, *Ajax* 646–7, "All things the long and countless lapse of time/Brings forth, displays, then hides once more in gloom."

guish literal from imaginative. His contemporary, Mimnermus, spoke of "time as long as a cubit," a phrase which definitely suggests that time was measurable; [9] and by the end of the sixth century there is clear evidence in a poem of Simonides for what we may properly term historic time, the sense of change in the passage of the years. Much earlier, an epitaph on the grave of Midas attributed to Cleobulus of Lindos had asserted that the sphinx over the grave would remain as long as water flowed, trees turned green, the moon came and the sun shone, the rivers flowed, and the sea came up on the beach. To this proclamation of static eternity Simonides rejoined, Who can praise Cleobulus in these views? "All these are subject to the Gods; but a stone, even mortal hands may break it. This is the rede of a fool." [1]

According to a later tale Simonides further engaged in eulogy of time at Olympia as most wise, for in it came the actions of learning and remembering. Not all Greeks, as we shall see below, could accept this idea of progress in time; the tale goes on to recount the rejoinder of a wise man present at Simonides' discourse, "O Simonides, is it not also true that in time we forget?" [2] Both Simonides and his critic, nonetheless, agreed that change was a product of time.

HISTORICAL TIME

Only when men comprehend, said Heidegger in a thoughtful essay on historical time, that the past is genuinely different from the present can a historical point of view develop. Sensitivity to this fact had clearly emerged by 500, though one must hasten to add a qualification. The conservative attitude of the

[9] Mimnermus fr. 2; as Accame, *Rivista di filologia* n.s. XXXIX (1961), pp. 383–84, points out, ὀλιγοχρόνιον also appears in Mimnermus (fr. 5); μικρὸν χρόνον is first found in Theognis 1273.
[1] Simonides fr. 48.
[2] Simplicius, *in Phys.* 4.13 (222b.17), 754.9.

Greeks, to wit, dulled the sharpness with which thinkers had transmuted their awareness of the great changes over the past two centuries into the concept that time produced alterations in society. Nonetheless time was beginning to assume that linear quality which Greek civilization passed on to later Western thought.[3]

The further idea that these changes, at least on the terrestrial level, were the result of human activity was also being voiced, as will appear more fully in Chapter IV. At this point we must assess what historical views of time the generations of Pindar, Aeschylus, and Herodotus inherited from the evolution of the period 700–500 B.C.; if the picture is not a simple one, this should not be surprising.

The nouns for "time" in Greek were by this time numerous. Beyond the terms for day, year, and seasons the word *chronos* represented the whole flow of time, but could be qualified by adjectives and participles to specify past or future. The word *aion* was later to have the significance of "eternity" or divine time for Platonic and subsequent thought, but down through Herodotus *aion* connoted primarily the duration of life, a generation of mankind. Another word to be charged with mystic meaning, *kairos*, commonly was applied to "the fitting occasion," a specific moment.[4] Apart from nouns, a great variety of particles, adverbs, and adjectives could be employed to

---

[3] Heidegger, *Zeitschrift für Philosophie*, CLXI (1916), p. 184. The modern linear view is summed up in Kant's statement, *Critique of Pure Reason* B154, tr. N. K. Smith, "Time itself we cannot represent, save . . . in the *drawing* of a straight line (which has to serve as the outer figurative representation of time)." R. G. Collingwood, "Some Perplexities about Time," *Aristotelian Society Proceedings*, XXVI (1926), pp. 135–50, notes modern attacks on this spatial concept of time; see Boman, *Hebrew Thought*, pp. 124–6, with the qualifications noted above, p. 28, n. 5.

[4] Degani, AIΩN; A. J. Festugière, "Le Sens philosophique du mot AIΩN," *Parola del Passato*, IV (1949), pp. 172–89. Doro Levi, "Il καιρός attraverso la letteratura greca," *Rendiconti della reale accademia dei Lincei*, 5. ser. XXXII (1923), pp. 260–81. See also Max Treu, "Griechische Ewigkeitswörter," *Glotta*, XLIII (1965), pp. 1–24; and Henry and Agathe Thornton, *Time and Style: A Psycho-linguistic Essay in Classical Literature* (London, 1962), pp. 9ff.

put action in the past or, less often, in the future. For the present the most common term was *nun*, "now."

To go further, let us consider in turn present, past, and future. Awareness that the present was a distinct stage, with its own characteristics, became ever sharper across the age of expansion. Hesiod's *Works and Days* had its origin in a real event, the injustice of his brother Perses, and Hesiod referred specifically to another contemporary occasion, the funeral games of king Amphidamas of Chalcis. The *Homeric Hymns*, while written during the next two centuries in an intentionally archaic fashion, looked into the future and commented on present conditions as being quite distinct from those of the legendary past. At the celebration of the Delian festival, it is said, girls sing of men and women of old, whose renown will never perish; the poet of this hymn to Apollo begs to be remembered in after time—the blind singer of Chios, "his lays are evermore supreme." [5] The Fourth Hymn, to Hermes, asserted that the three hides of Hermes were *now* visible, "a long, long time after all this"; the Second, to Demeter, alluded to aspects of current worship at Eleusis; and two others, those to Athena (Eleven) and Demeter (Thirteen), invoked the deities to keep "this city safe."

In Archilochus, Alcaeus, and Sappho presentism is an overwhelming force; and we begin also to find references to recent events as useful examples, such as the fall of Magnesia in Callinus and Archilochus. This calamity, together with the fall of Colophon and Smyrna, was later picked up by Theognis of Megara as a warning to his beloved Cyrnus; Theognis also engaged in a bitter attack on the Cypselids of nearby Corinth.[6] Both the internal and the external contentions of the city-states did much to make their citizens politically conscious of the present and recent past.

The historic past, which was real and significant, required

[5] *Homeric Hymn* 3, 156–60, 166–75; 4, 125–6.
[6] Theognis 603ff., 1101ff., 891ff. Of the references to wars with the Medes (764ff., 775ff.) the latter at least apparently is later.

by 500 B.C. chronological means for measuring its flow; for careful chronology is, after all, a significant end product of the awareness of time as historical. Xenophanes dated his youth by the time "when the Mede came," and Hecataeus seems to have looked back over earlier times as a series of generations; scholars, however, find it difficult to settle how many years he or any other generation counter may have assigned to one lifetime.[7] In political life, on the other hand, very specific measurement by years had become necessary, though only on the level of each state. As noted earlier the Greek *poleis* had many different systems for dating months and adjusted them to the solar year in various fashions; so too each developed a list of years, reckoning in Sparta by kings, at Argos by priestesses of Hera, or at Athens by the archons. This latter list, of which we have fragments from a copy set up probably in the Agora late in the fifth century, began in 683 B.C.[8] Herodotus could employ these local schemes to gain chronological correlations; his contemporary Hellanicus and later scholars were to go further in establishing a Panhellenic pattern of temporal sequences.

These lists are a very tangible illustration of the belief that the present, itself a real condition, was the product of time in the past, which had changed the physical world about mankind as well as marking the alterations of human society. Far in man's background lay the world of myth, which the Greeks accepted as true and celebrated in sculpture, pottery, dithyrambs, and other forms of art and literature. This was a closed era which did not melt gradually into the historic age even

[7] Xenophanes fr. 22; according to Aulus Gellius, *Attic Nights* 3.11, he thought Homer older than Hesiod. On Hecataeus see below, p. 114, n. 4. Generations: W. den Boer, *Laconian Studies* (Amsterdam, 1954); Fordyce Mitchel, "Herodotus' Use of Genealogical Chronology," *Phoenix*, X (1956), pp. 48–69; D. W. Prakken, *Studies in Greek Genealogical Chronology* (Lancaster, Pa., 1943).

[8] D. W. Bradeen, "The Fifth-Century Archon List," *Hesperia*, XXXII (1963), pp. 187–208. General chronology: Wilhelm Kubitschek, *Grundriss der antiken Zeitrechnung* (Munich, 1928); Elias Bickerman, *Chronologie* (2d ed.; Leipzig, 1963).

though eventually efforts were to be made to relate its events chronologically to those of real time. Within that period just behind the world of 500 B.C., the age of expansion, change had occurred on so wide a scale that men could not ignore it, as we observed in the preceding section; both Herodotus and also Thucydides, in his opening section on earlier Greek history, were to describe this change in historical terms. The major theoretical statement of this awareness which can be placed before 500 is Xenophanes' assertion, "Truly the gods have not revealed to mortals all things from the beginning; but mortals by long seeking discover what is better." [9]

A concomitant of this view is the effort to assign inventions to specific individuals. Solon thus proclaimed Arion the inventor of the dithyramb, and Anaximander attributed foreign arts to historic personages.[1] In the fifth century, to look ahead briefly, the quest for the inventor of arts and crafts was a frequent pastime which produced, by the end of the century, an essay specifically on the topic by the sophist Critias. To a limited degree this search may have facilitated a historical attitude, but its area of interest was more in the cultural than in the political sphere.

A parallel line of development was the crystallization of a theory of human progress, which was widely known in Athens in the age of Pericles and thereafter. Aeschylus' *Prometheus Bound* contains a praise of man's cultural progress; an even more famous paean, which expresses a clear concept of progress, is that inserted by Sophocles in his *Antigone,* "a kind of

[9] Xenophanes fr. 18. It should, however, be noted that this fragment does not suggest real change, but rather the discovery by men of the real situation; so Protagoras (in Plato, *Protagoras* 316D) can argue that the sophistic art is really ancient, but men of old hid it behind a veiled appearance.
[1] Cf. commentary by Johannes Diaconus on Hermogenes, H. Rabe, *Rheinisches Museum,* LXIII (1908), p. 150; Battegazzore and Untersteiner, *Sofisti,* IV, pp. 252ff. In general, Adolf Kleingüthner, "ΠΡΩΤΟΣ ΕΥΡΕΤΑΣ: Untersuchungen zur Geschichte einer Fragestellung," *Philologus,* Supplementband XXVI, Heft 1 (1933); K. Thraede, "Das Lob des Erfinders," *Rheinisches Museum,* CV (1962), pp. 158–86.

vision of man as truly *homo sapiens*, in control of his own history and moulding his own environment." [2] The much later historian Diodorus picked up a view of early human development as progress with which he began his history of the world; as elaborated, this sequence appears Hellenistic, but very probably it took its root from fifth-century speculation. Even Plato, who displayed little interest in earthly time, could observe at one point that "doubtless the change was not made all in a moment, but little by little, during a very long period of time." [3] But the most remarkable and conscious manifestation of the idea was the Hippocratic treatise *On Ancient Medicine*. From of old, this essay asserts, medicine has been a skill, and so its discoveries "over a long period" have been numerous and of good quality; thanks to its sound method others will be found in the future.[4] Thus specifically man's diet has been developed by experimentation, and new discoveries are still made "now" by masters of the gymnasia and of exercises.

This mode of thought must interest particularly modern generations, imbued until recently with an almost mystic faith in inevitable progress; but in the context of Greek views about the relations of past to present it was a side shoot which had little general appeal. Even in assigning the discovery of techniques and customs the Greeks insisted on thinking of the

[2] E. A. Havelock, *The Liberal Temper in Greek Politics* (New Haven, 1957), p. 69; W. K. C. Guthrie, *In the Beginning* (London, 1957), chaps. v–vi. Among the fifth-century statements see Aeschylus, *Prometheus Bound* 447ff.; Sophocles, *Antigone* 332ff.; Euripides, *Suppliants* 196ff.; Critias fr. 25 (Battegazzore and Untersteiner, *Sofisti*, IV, pp. 308ff.); Moschion fr. 6; Plato, *Protagoras* 320C–2D (Untersteiner, *Sofisti*, I, pp. 97ff. and 23ff.).
[3] Plato, *Laws* 3.678B (tr. Jowett). On Diodorus 1.8, see W. Spoerri, *Späthellenistische Berichte über Welt, Kultur und Götter. Untersuchungen zu Diodor von Sizilien* (Basel, 1959); Guthrie, *Greek Philosophy*, II, p. 210.
[4] *On Ancient Medicine* (ed. Heiberg) 37–8; Harold W. Miller, "*Techne* and Discovery in *On Ancient Medicine*," *Transactions of the American Philological Association*, LXXXVI (1955), pp. 51–62.

gods.[5] While Terpander was probably the inventor of the seven-stringed lyre, tradition spoke also of Hermes; and the praises of earthly advance delivered by the sophists, no less than that of Aeschylus, were not always connected directly with human, as against divine, sources.

From Hesiod on, the Greeks were far from convinced that the present age of iron was a progress over the past. In their own lives they looked candidly and coldly at the ravages of time, and were all too aware of the short span of life which most men could expect; the vicious struggles of political life and the slowly changing patterns of economic and social existence could scarcely inspirit them to optimism. Time took place, yes, but commonly its passage seemed to mean decay and destruction. Philosophers generalized this course in cyclical terms; as Aristotle reports, the common opinion was that human affairs form a circle.[6]

Such views were powerful; still, one must not forget that some observers were unable thus to simplify the pattern of change which they observed. The Pythagorean doctor Alcmaeon of Croton early in the fifth century doubted whether each cycle came back exactly to the same point; much later the atomist Leucippus bluntly denied that time moved cyclically rather than on a line.[7] What historians thought of the matter must concern us later.

[5] Kleingüthner, *Philologus*, Supplementband XXVI, Heft 1 (1933), pp. 22, 29; Lesky, *History of Greek Literature*, pp. 128–9.
[6] Aristotle, *Physics* 4.14 (223b.24ff), also quoted in *Problemata* 17.3 (916a.29), which argues from cyclical movement in the heavens to human affairs; Guthrie, *Greek Philosophy*, I, pp. 388–90.
[7] Alcmaeon fr. 2; Aristotle, *Problemata* 17.3 (916a.24–26); Guthrie, *Greek Philosophy*, I, pp. 351–3 (and on Leucippus, *Greek Philosophy*, II, p. 429). Goldschmidt, *Le Système stoïcien*, notes later philosophic awareness that time could be conceived either in a circle or on a line; cf. Degani, ΑΙΩΝ pp. 121–3, on Anaxagoras. In general see A. Diès, *Le Cycle mystique* (Paris, 1909); Ch. Mugler, *Deux Thèmes de la cosmologie grecque: devenir cyclique et pluralité des mondes* (Paris, 1953); J. F. Callahan, *Four Views of Time in Ancient Philosophy* (Cambridge, Mass., 1948).

No one turned to gaze into the future with enthusiasm. The most common observation about the future, to be found repeatedly in Pindar, was that it was unpredictable; and always, when referred to, the future was tied directly to the emotions of the speaker or writer. No classic historian closed his work by looking into what was yet to come; and Greek verbal forms for the future did not contain the suggestion that something would *really* happen.[8] Only as Christian theology became dominant did the future begin to play a significant role in its eschatological significance. This doctrine has not been of great value to history proper, but it must be said that the limited interest of the Greeks in the future seriously restricted their views of the past; for concern with the human future has often been a driving force in historical exploration of the human past.

In the end it remains amazing that the Greeks, subjected to heavy stresses in their advance from a very traditional level of life, could develop even the fundamental basis for a historical appreciation of their progress. Their strongly religious temperament and inbred conservatism help to explain how partial was the dominance of that temporal awareness which had emerged by 500.

How would a Greek thinker at this time have defined *chronos* itself? To those of philosophical bent the word would be likely to have had a cyclical connotation; even so time was a measurable attribute for philosophers no less than for poets in their meters.[9] Mystics and poets generally sensed *chronos* as a personified force, moving man against his will and not always in desirable courses. To a few at least *chronos* brought with it the idea of a regular passage of time from past to

[8] K. Reinhardt, in *Herodot*, p. 324; van Groningen, *In the Grip of the Past*, pp. 109–11. On the role of the future in law see L. Gernet, "Le Temps dans les formes archaïques du droit," *Journal de psychologie*, LIII (1956), pp. 379–406.
[9] On metrical time see L. E. Rossi, *Metrica e critica stilistica* (Rome, 1963), pp. 65–6, 93–8.

present. In Aristotle's abstract words, "time is the number of movement"; and later in the treatise *De Caelo* he sharply distinguished the nonmaterial world from that of nature in the matter of generation and change. Again in the *Physics* he stated that "time is 'number of movement in respect to the before and after,' and is continuous"; in this discussion he treated of time as a chronological measurement.[1]

These were the views of a man of the fourth century, which had become rather fully impregnated with a historical appreciation of time; but even by the early fifth century conscious comprehension of time as change was rising in arts and letters. One recent student of Greek sculpture thus casts the difference between archaic and classical styles partly in temporal terms; whereas motion in the archaic era was an accidental accessory, statues of the classic period stood in real space and had an inner capacity for movement.[2] Even more illuminating is the work of the great poet Pindar, whose praises of aristocratic athletes, unlike the Homeric epics, were firmly set in time.

Very close to Pindar's view of time was that of Herodotus, who was to be able to take chains of events in very distant areas and link them firmly together along a straight line. The involutions and inversions of which Herodotus, no less than Pindar, was capable have sometimes baffled modern observers, inured to the tyranny of historical chronology; but of the basic point, that Herodotus saw the history of the past as setting the world of the present, there can be no doubt. Thereafter came Thucydides, who moved sharply toward a "dynamic" view of development.[3]

[1] Aristotle, *De Caelo* 1.9 (279a.15) (tr. Ross), 3.1 (298b.13ff); *Physics* 4.11 (220a.24–5) (tr. Ross); see also *Metaphysics* 1.5.11 (986b.17–18); *de generatione et corruptione* 1 (325a.13); and generally Paul F. Conen, "Die Zeittheorie des Aristoteles," *Zetemata* XXXV (1964).
[2] Karl Schefold, *Griechische Kunst als religiöses Phänomen* (Hamburg, 1959), pp. 75–6, 79; cf. too his remarks, pp. 132–3, on the representation of the visible world in Greek art.
[3] See especially H. Strasburger, *Die Wesensbestimmung der Geschichte durch die antike Geschichtsschreibung* (Wiesbaden, 1966), pp. 58–9.

77

CHAPTER 4

MAN

AND THE STATE

ⅬⅬⅬⅬⅬⅬⅬⅬⅬⅬⅬⅬⅬⅬⅬⅬⅬⅬⅬⅬⅬⅬⅬⅬⅬ

IF THE DIMENSIONS of history are space and time, its subject is man. More precisely historians portray men operating together or at cross-purposes within a conscious political structure. The old distinction between prehistory as resting on physical remains and history as the stage of written records, produced by civilized societies, has now lost much of its value, for archaeological materials have become more extensive and are often susceptible to delicate analysis; nor can modern accounts of the ancient Aegean properly overlook its Minoan and Mycenaean phases, in which writing was used at least to a limited degree. Yet it remains true that history, as a written account of earlier times, developed in the Greek world only well after the appearance of organized city-states, and depended on that evolution.

No aspect of archaic civilization can be treated adequately if one leaves the *polis* entirely out of the story. The tiny political units which jelled out of the "peoples" of earlier Greece sought to emphasize from the beginning the unity of their citizenry. Each city-state felt itself protected by some particular god or goddess, whose shrine soon became as majestic a temple as the citizens could afford to build; and the earthly ideal of the *polis* was even-handed justice under a rule

Prothesis scene from Dipylon amphora (National Museum 200, Athens).

PLATE I · *The World of Homer*

(a) Dionysius in his ship, cup by Exekias (Antikensammlung 2044, Munich).

(b) Youth from Sunium (National Museum 3344, Athens).

PLATE II · *The Sixth Century*

Laconian cup (Cabinet des Médailles 4899 [2707], Paris).

PLATE III · *The Arcesilaus Cup*

Amphora by Myson (Musée du Louvre G 197, Paris).

PLATE IV · *Croesus on His Pyre*

*) Scythian archer, plate by
pictetus (British Museum
135, London).*

) Persians, from Attic vase c.450 (Staatliche Museen F 3156, Berlin). NOTE: *These two figures
e not contiguous on the vase, and so are separated.*

PLATE V · *Scythians and Persians*

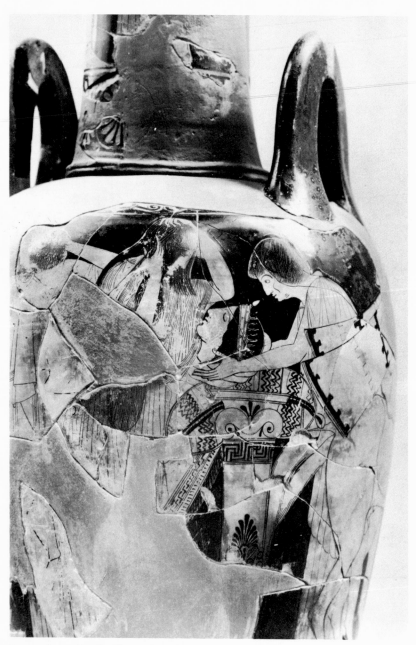

Loutrophoros by Kleophrades painter (National Museum 1170, Athens).

PLATE VI · *Death in the Fifth Century*

(a) Battle of gods and giants, from the
Siphnian frieze (Delphi Museum).

(b) Heracles and the priests of Busiris,
pelike by Pan painter (National Museum 9683, Athens).

PLATE VII · *Narrative in the Sixth and Fifth Centuries*

Relief from the Acropolis (Acropolis Museum 695, Athens).

PLATE VIII · *The Mourning Athena*

of law. The Greek city-state has well been termed a hothouse, in which intellectual development was greatly stimulated and in which intense political life flourished. Since the kings of earlier days generally withered away as the *polis* developed and Greek religion lacked a powerful priesthood, the citizens of each small, yet completely independent unit were free to become aware of themselves, in Aristotle's famous phrase, as "political animals." [1] The internal development of these states as well as their external clashes undoubtedly served as one root for an interest in the past as historical; the development also produced a variety of physical testimony which could furnish anchors for that interest.

While considering carefully these political spurs toward historical products, we must not interpret the city-state entirely in terms of the modern nation-state, sharply defined and firmly organized as a focus for the ideals and practical needs of its members. Although the *polis* emerged toward the end of the eighth century, it developed only slowly across the archaic period both with respect to its machinery of government and in gaining the loyalty of its citizens. On the one side the ties of aristocrats stretched far beyond the bounds of any one state, which nobles could divide in their contentions; on the other side parochial social and religious groupings, as in clans, local cult societies, and the like, yielded reluctantly to the overriding patriotism which we consider a mark of classic Athens or of the ideal states of Plato and Aristotle. The first historian, Herodotus, may speak at times of Athenians or Lacedaemonians as conscious entities, but his accounts of noble feuds and wandering Greeks should be ample warning against any depiction of the city-states of sixth-century Greece as monolithic, all-encompassing blocks.

---

[1] Aristotle, *Politics* 1.1.9 (1253a.2–3). Victor Ehrenberg, *The Greek State* (New York: Norton paperback, 1964), gives a bibliography; some aspects appear in my essays, "The Early Greek City-State," *Parola del Passato,* XII (1957), pp. 97–108, and "The Decline of the Early Greek Kings," *Historia,* X (1961), pp. 129–38.

The rise of the *polis* therefore is not a sufficient factor *in itself* to explain the origins of a historical appreciation of man.[2] During the archaic era, admittedly, the citizens of the more advanced communities coalesced into a conscious audience, which eventually came to support historical as well as philosophical and tragic explorations; but also they became self-moving human figures. The ability of the Greeks to combine the first great humanistic outlook with a deeply pious belief in the will of the gods was a remarkable phenomenon; what must concern us in the last section of the present chapter is the incipient exploration of the idea that human beings caused, or were responsible, for their actions. This too was a necessary ingredient for a truly historical outlook.

THE RISE OF POLITICAL LIFE

Historical awareness of the past extended only dimly back from the fifth century across the archaic period, especially as regarded the seventh century; to write a continuous political history of the period is thus logically impossible. Still, bits and pieces survive in one form or another to suggest that external relations among the city-states and also constitutional developments within a particular *polis* did become ever more connected and significant in a historical sense.

Externally the first war of which we have some notice, as distinct from cattle-raiding or simple movement of tribes, was the Lelantine War, waged between Chalcis and Eretria over a tiny, disputed plain about 700 B.C. If later reconstructions can be trusted even in limited degree, a number of other states were drawn into this conflict through their ties to one of the two parties.[3] Thereafter various wars and the expansiveness of

[2] Contra, Chatelet, *La Naissance de l'histoire.*
[3] The evidence is given in A. R. Burn, "The So-called 'Trade Leagues' in Early Greek History and the Lelantine War," *Journal of Hellenic Studies,* XLIX (1929), pp. 14–37.

aggressive states were remembered, even though the greatest warlord of the seventh century, Pheidon of Argos, cannot be tied down chronologically with any certainty. From about 600 B.C., however, the foreign relations of both Sparta and Athens, and also to some extent of Corinth and other states, were sufficiently meaningful for men of the fifth and fourth centuries that they preserved enough testimony to permit the construction of modern accounts.

In general this was a period in which the city-states assumed the territorial form they normally held thereafter. A truly historical outlook was not likely to emerge totally *de novo* in so confused an era, where the boundary between noble feuds and state action was still vague.[4] Nevertheless the technique of appealing to the mythical past to justify a present territorial possession or to warrant a war of revenge began to appear in the sixth century. The one interpolation in the *Iliad* whose source we know, for example, is the line 2.558, which assigns Salamis to Athens in the Trojan period as a reflection of the sixth-century contention between Megara and Athens over its ownership. Again, when king Cleomenes of Sparta came to Athens in an effort to expel Clisthenes in 508 and was barred by a priestess from worshiping Athena on the Acropolis on the grounds that he was a Dorian, he was able to rejoin with the equally "historical" statement that his ancestry was Achaean.[5] Memory of earlier times, in sum, was coming to have practical utility and patriotic meaning, even if it was couched largely in genealogical and epic connections.

Internally as well the archaic era was one of great confusion, as the changing economic and social conditions of the nascent city-states brought tensions and injustices. Although upheavals and revolutions did not cease with the classic era, a long framework of constitutional change had by that point

[4] Starr, *Origins*, pp. 324–48; Heuss, *Antike und Abendland*, II (1946), pp. 42, 53–7; Victor Martin, *La vie internationale dans la Grèce des cités* (*VIᵉ–IVᵉ s. av. J.-C.*) (Paris, 1940).
[5] Herodotus 5.72.3.

produced a fairly extensive and coordinated political machinery and also more conscious political attitudes. The emergent *polis* of the seventh century was a far simpler, inchoate structure than students of Greek government commonly realize; but particularly in the case of Attica we can follow the increasing centralization of political and religious authority at the political center of Athens itself, and can occasionally see the rivalries of aristocratic clans and less privileged elements through the careers of Solon, Pisistratus and his sons, and Clisthenes.[6] Here too memories and precedents gradually became implanted, to be tapped first by Herodotus and Hellanicus as an explanation for the foundations of the fifth century.

The elaboration of the machinery of government demanded precision of statement to an unwonted degree in financial, constitutional and other records; the product was physical evidence of many types. Treaties of alliance between states were carved on stone or engraved in bronze tablets, the earliest of which so far found date from about the middle of the sixth century and were set up at Olympia, while in coinage there appears to be a commemoration of a treaty of alliance between Chalcis and Thebes in 506.[7] The laws of a state also needed to be exhibited publicly, particularly when they had been revised to cope with some internal problem. At Athens the laws of Solon were placed on *kyrbes* or wooden panels, and stone copies of laws, as at Chios, have survived. The institution of ostracism, when introduced at Athens early in the fifth century, produced a quite different harvest in the recent excavations of the Agora, which uncovered piles of

---

[6] C. Hignett, *History of the Athenian Constitution to the End of the Fifth Century B.C.* (Oxford, 1952), pp. 34–8.

[7] See my essay on "The Awakening of the Greek Historical Spirit and Early Greek Coinage," forthcoming in *Numismatic Chronicle* (especially n. 18). Treaties: H. Bengtson, *Die Staatsverträge des Altertums,* II (Munich, 1962), nos. 110 (= Tod, *GHI,* I, no. 5), 111, 120; Bengtson gives others attested only in our literary evidence. Law of Chios: Tod, *GHI,* I, no. 1.

sherds marked with the names of Themistocles and other fifth-century Attic politicians; though later than 500 these masses of *ostraka* are perhaps our most impressive visual testimony to the rise of "political" man on a wide scale. To what extent the city-states had public records offices is a debatable matter, even for Athens in the fifth century; but I find it difficult to doubt that at least a rudimentary collection of papyrus copies of laws, financial accounts, and other materials existed—and probably in a greater abundance than the haphazard survival of stone and bronze versions suggests.[8]

Such by-products of the processes of government were not specifically intended as historical materials, and especially when hidden away in primitive archives seem only rarely to have been used by historians. Other objects, however, of many types were set up in sanctuaries and public places for motives which we must account very close to historical in intent. By the sixth century many cities must have had lists of eponymous officials, and this chronological aid was carved on stone at Athens by the later fifth century if not before. Victory in battle required commemoration in many ways. On the battlefield itself the victors might erect a trophy; in the shrines at home and at the great international centers other testimonials were dedicated, such as archaic spearpoints on the Acropolis at Athens and helmets at Olympia by Hiero of Syracuse and by Miltiades after Marathon.[9] These dedications, almost cryptic in their brief inscriptions, served as anchors for the oral memory of great events. By 500 B.C. epigrams were beginning to be carved on stone bases; the earliest of which we have fragments commemorates the Athenian victory over Boeotia and Chalcis in 506, and it is worth noting that Herodotus

[8] Bradeen, *Hesperia*, XXXII (1963), p. 205, after Thompson; contra, Hignett, *Athenian Constitution*, pp. 12–17 et al.
[9] G. C. Picard, *Les Trophées romaines* (Paris, 1957), pp. 13–64; Karl Woelcke, "Beiträge zur Geschichte des Tropaions," *Bonner Jahrbücher*, CXX (1911), pp. 127–235; Tod, *GHI*, I, no. 22 (cf. nos. 6–9); Richter, *Portraits of the Greeks*, figs. 390 and 391.

copied this publicly visible record.[1] Other epigrams, in greater numbers, were the product of the Persian conflict, as we shall see in Chapter VI.

In sculpture the earliest statues bearing human names are those of Cleobis and Biton at Delphi, from about 600. More significant historically was the commemoration at Athens of Harmodius and Aristogeiton, the tyrant slayers. Their statues by Antenor were erected in the Agora soon after 510, the first such representations in a secular public place as distinguished from a religious sanctuary and the only ones down to the time of Conon (the early fourth century).[2] After the Persian invasion of Attica, when the original group was removed to Persia, the Athenians felt it so important to have a public memorial of the tyrannicide that they commissioned new statues by Critios and Nesiotes. Soon thereafter, probably about 460, is dated a statue of Themistocles, the earliest representation of a statesman of which we know; a Roman copy of its head survives from Ostia.[3] Panaenus' painting of Marathon in the Stoa Poikile included Miltiades, Callimachus, and other Athenian and Persian figures; but one may doubt if they were endowed with specific characteristics any further than were Arcesilaus of

[1] Tod, *GHI*, I, nos. 12, 43; most of what survives is from the restored copy *c*.445, but a tiny fragment of the original is extant; Herodotus 5.77.
[2] Sture Brunnsåker, *The Tyrant-Slayers of Kritios and Nesiotes* (Lund, 1955); Richter, *The Portraits of the Greeks*, fig. xvii–ix; A. J. Podlecki, "The Political Significance of the Athenian 'Tyrannicide'-Cult," *Historia*, XV (1966), pp. 129–41; below, p. 122, n. 2. Conon: Demosthenes, *Against Leptines* 70. On the *skolia* in honor of the tyrannicides (Athenaeus 15.695a–b), see V. Ehrenberg, "Das Harmodioslied," *Wiener Studien*, LXIX (1956), pp. 57–69; Bowra, *Greek Lyric Poetry*, pp. 393–6.
[3] Richter, *Portraits of the Greeks*, pp. 31–2, 99; the statue of Miltiades preserved in a Ravenna head, she places *c*.450 (pp. 96–7). Others, however, would consider the Themistocles head as a Hellenistic creation, and historically one must wonder if 460 would have been a suitable period for its erection. See generally Anton Hekler, *Bildnisse berühmter Griechen*, ed. Helga von Heintze (3d ed.; Berlin, 1962), and B. Schweitzer, *Studien zur Entstehung des Porträts bei den Griechen* (Leipzig, 1940). On the Stoa Poikile, see below, p. 122, n. 3; for depictions of poets on vases, p. 122, n. 2.

Cyrene and Croesus of Lydia in the vases shown on Plates III and IV.

THE AUDIENCE OF THE *POLIS*

Historically, portraits in stone or in paintings and vases are important because they reveal the public demand for memorials of persons famous for political, military, or poetic achievement. The same force had its role in prompting the compositions of the first histories; as Shotwell observed,

> It is not so much the long procession of the centuries which produces the historian as the need to convince one's contemporaries of the truth of what one tells. The mere possession of a mighty past is of less value than a critical audience.[4]

The importance of such an audience may easily be missed by modern students, accustomed to think of Herodotus' history in terms of a book which they read in their individual studies; but actually most Greek authors, including the Father of History, composed their works in the first instance for oral delivery. Neither writer nor artist in ancient Greece created, as a rule, solely for their own satisfaction; always they had in mind auditors whose interests and qualities did much to shape and to spur their work. Any assessment of Greek culture must keep in the foreground not only the aims of its creators but also the imperious dictation of their far from passive audience.

This existed on several levels. One was Panhellenic, exemplified particularly in the largely aristocratic assemblages at Olympia and other international shrines. Here states dedicated memorials of their victories; here Gorgias, Isocrates, and others in later days presented their ideas in orations just as much earlier, at the Delian festival to Apollo, "the long robed Io-

[4] Shotwell, *History of Ancient History*, p. 158.

nians gather in your honor with their children and shy wives, mindful, they delight you with boxing and dancing and song, so often as they hold their gathering." But one might appeal to this level more generally, as did Pindar in several odes. So too did Herodotus, for his great recital of the Persian Wars was certainly directed at the Greeks as a whole.[5] Nonetheless the first reading of his work took place before an audience in *one* city-state, that of Athens; the basic unit for literature, as for politics, was the *polis*. What then were the qualities of this audience?

In the *polis* the free adult male had a political role which tended to become ever more active and conscious across the archaic era; in that development the concept of individual rights and responsibilities was fixed as an underlying principle in all later Western political thought. Already in the seventh century the vehement outbursts of the poet Archilochus made manifest the political involvement of the conscious citizen, an involvement so intense and bitter as to produce now assassinations and civil wars, now such scurrilous attacks on opponents as those of the poet Alcaeus. Life in the *polis* was as vigorous and mercurial as that of the Italian communes in the Renaissance.

The processes of daily living as well as of political activity were highly public. The state was often called "the common thing," and its community was expressed and directed by a babble of words.[6] The simple forms of housing, together with the relatively mild Mediterranean climate, encouraged men to be out-of-doors, at least by day; when true urban centers developed, they seem always to have had an open meeting place (the *agora*) for business, for political action, and for exchanging gossip. Just as the sun beat down hot on a summer midday, so public opinion vented itself fiercely and openly in a city-state; and a receptive, quick audience emerged, the needs and demands of which had to be satisfied by sculptors,

[5] *Homeric Hymn*, 3, 147–50; for Pindar and Herodotus see Chapter VI.
[6] Vernant, *Les Origines de la pensée grecque*, pp. 36–46.

by poets, and eventually by historians no less than by political
leaders.

The roots of this audience went back to the assembly of
warriors, lolling after feasts in the shadowy megaron of a king
and listening to the lays of Homer. Yet the mockery and
savage assaults of Archilochus had the public as their audience; the maiden choruses of Alcman sang at open Spartan
festivals. Dithyrambs, hymns, and the Homeric epics as well
were probably recited or sung in many cities. This double
aspect, a select gathering and a large communal group, must
always be kept in mind when one considers precisely what the
term "audience" might mean on any specific occasion.

The bitter outcry of Hesiod against injustice, thus, seems
designed for the elders of the market place. "Criticism," comments Jaeger, "is freely directed at the conduct of their fellows, even at the distinguished lords, and 'what the people
say' (φήμη) is of decisive importance for the reputation and
career of the ordinary man." [7] Such lyric poets as Alcaeus and
Sappho, on the other hand, addressed themselves to small,
aristocratic groups. Taken generally, the audience which poets,
philosophers, and sculptors of the archaic period had in mind
as their arbiters and judges was probably the aristocratic level
of Greek society.

This leisured class developed an ever more conscious stand-
ard of values in the period as a base for the later Roman and
Western aristocratic ethos; it also was remarkably receptive to
innovations. The swift, unrelenting exploration of man and his
world which produced the triumphs of archaic sculpture and
philosophy owed much to the aristocrats who carried on the
bold, free spirit of the Homeric hero. To what extent, however, a coterie or *hetairia* of aristocrats would in itself ever
have produced a truly historical outlook, as it quaffed its wine
amid pleasant talk, is problematical. True, its members de-

[7] Jaeger, *Paideia*, I, p. 91 (on Archilochus, pp. 163–72); Hesiod, *Works
and Days* 3–4, and *Theogony* 430. Cf. the picture of the elders in the
market in *Iliad* 18.503–5.

lighted in boasting of their ancestors and kept in mind long genealogical tables; in Theognis we can see the interest of such circles in personal matters and the expression of individual judgments. But the expression was biased rather than objective; and the interest was not likely to lead on to reasoned, continuous surveys of public development—the cantankerous Xenophanes has even left on record his objection to tales of civil strife.[8] From the memories of this level Herodotus might draw, but the spirit animating his history had other and wider roots.

The masses nowhere enjoyed full political rights during the period down to 508, but this exclusion did not keep them totally silent. Sometimes their babble obviously angered the aristocrats: Phocylides warned that a *hetairos* should consider with his fellows what the "citizens" mutter in their ears, and Mimnermus burst out that "the pitiless citizens will speak good and ill of you." In opposition to the commonalty Pythagorean societies sought to keep their knowledge secret, and closed groups continued from Alcaeus' time far down in Greek history to enspirit their members by antipopular songs and speeches or even to plot revolution to restore ancestral constitutions.[9]

All this, however, suggests the power of the community. In any age one must be skeptical of efforts to distinguish the "opinion makers" or arbiters of taste too far from society as a whole; save in the narrowest of developments major currents of thought or belief will be shared alike by intellectual and nonintellectual segments of a population. Particularly was this true in ancient Greece, where the enduring ideal of the *polis* was that of the bond of all its citizens.

[8] Xenophanes fr. 1. See also Anacreon fr. 96; Phocylides fr. 14; Theognis 467ff., 531–4, 757ff., 983ff., etc. Yet, as Bowra, *Greek Lyric Poetry*, pp. 373ff., shows, the Attic drinking songs which have survived do have considerable political links.

[9] Phocylides fr. 5; Mimnermus fr. 7; Snell, *Gymnasium*, LXV (1958), p. 51; M. T. Cardini, *Pitagorici: testimonianze e frammenti*, I (Florence, 1958), pp. 88–92.

Modern students of sociology would undoubtedly seek to break down the public opinion of such a body into various pressure elements or judgment-forming centers; and, had we the information, divisions in this audience certainly should be carefully analyzed. Yet the practical effects of factionalism and the growingly conscious distinction of an aristocratic social pattern were in the end minor; fundamentally the citizens of each *polis*, a few thousand adult males, were an interreacting community, justly called "the Athenians" or "the Lacedaemonians" as political entities.

This public audience was active rather than passive in its reactions. By the fifth century there are open statements that one must make oneself clear to the "ordinary people," [1] but earlier evidence exists for a general body politic. In the seventh century Tyrtaeus had poured out his military appeals to the public opinion of Sparta, and promised that the memory of brave men would last "among men." [2] Even more impressive recognition of the commonalty came in the life and activities of Solon. From the time when he uttered his battle cry to regain Salamis before the public Solon addressed himself to the people rather than speaking just for himself. Well aware of the drive of his fellow citizens for wealth, which sundered rich and poor, he "stood with a strong shield thrown before the both sorts, and would have neither to prevail unrighteously over the other." In Solon's eyes the ills of the community might be ascribed in the first degree to unjust leaders, but ultimately responsibility was collective: "So cometh the common evil into every house, and the street-doors will no longer keep it out; it leapeth the high hedge and surely findeth a man, for all he may go hide himself in his chamber."

Insofar as we can probe the period before 500 B.C., Athens may have been somewhat distinct in its intentional emphasis

[1] *On Ancient Medicine* 37 (Heiberg).
[2] Tyrtaeus fr. 9; cf. Solon fr. 9. In Callinus fr. 1 the same idea of popular glory seems to apply only to the *present* generation. The following quotations of Solon are from frr. 5 and 3.

on the unity of the state. Solon's broad spirit seemed almost lost in the bitter struggles following his partial reforms, but the first solution to these intestinal conflicts was the tyranny of Pisistratus and his sons, who sought to beautify the urban center of Athens, to reduce the power of the clans, and to unify the citizenry through magnificent festivals, such as the Panathenaea, and through encouragement of patriotism. On this basis the reformer Clisthenes was thereafter able to reorganize the Athenian constitution in 508/7 to lodge political power firmly in the hands of the general assembly.

To what extent the growing commercial and industrial classes of Athens contributed to or spurred political developments is not as clear as modern students, impressed by the recent rise of the *bourgeoisie,* sometimes suggest; for most men still lived by agriculture in 500. Here too, however, the small farmers had gained a more secure position thanks to the debt reforms of Solon and to the Pisistratid redistribution of lands, together with the increasing attention to production of olives and grapes. Whether rural or urban, the citizen body of Athens by 500 formed a general audience of significant weight, where men not only voted but also passed judgments on cultural matters; the fact that aristocrats still provided the outward leadership across the fifth century cannot mask the abundant evidence of an independent folk.

To say that this city-state provided the one and only audience ready to listen to historical accounts of its present position would be much too rash a conclusion; indeed the Athenian public of the early fifth century, accustomed to a host of divine and epic figures in sculpture, on red-figured vases, and on the tragic stage, did not think very largely in historical terms. Yet it is perhaps not accidental that this citizenry desired public memorials of its great deeds; and, though historians appeared elsewhere in the fifth century, both Herodotus and Hellanicus were drawn to Athens. Exactly who formed the audience for Herodotus' public readings we do not know;

but various bits of evidence, to be considered in Chapter VI, suggest a general reaction, and favorable at that, to his work.

HUMAN SELF-AWARENESS

During the archaic period the Greeks not only became aware of themselves as members of a communal political group, but also gained a sense of individual significance. This was a great step, which necessarily commands a large place in any modern discussion of early Greek civilization; here I need only touch upon some aspects which throw light on the extent to which the responsibility for human actions came to be lodged in men's own decisions.

The answer to this latter problem is not a simple one. Even today human causation, in the sense that human beings voluntarily produce their own history, is not as widespread a belief as historical manuals suggest; for often blind, superhuman forces—such as imperialism, the ineluctable side of Marxist dialectic, the Challenge and Response of Toynbee, and so on—have stalked across the pages of historical studies, moving men like puppets. God no longer reaches down His inexorable hand, but the moving finger of History must still have its guide. In early Greece the gods, sometimes frightening, sometimes benign, were visible masters of human destinies; what we must look to find is a matter of nuances, tendencies, and partial assertions of human freedom of will. This was essential for the rise of a historical outlook—if history explains to us the world in which we live there must be a sense of the human part in making this world.

In many ways the freest individuals in Greece before the fourth century were the Homeric heroes. Politically they did not yet suffer the yoke of the city-state, and obeyed their war chieftains only as their own will dictated; the trammels of magic, of superstition, or of conventional beliefs were singularly lacking, especially in the *Iliad*. Even to the gods the heroes hearkened only if they wished, though they admitted, "What the gods command you, do, then the gods will listen to *you*." [3] Withal, the men of the *Iliad* and the *Odyssey* ascribed both their folly and their strength to the Olympian gods and, behind them, to all-powerful Fate.

This ascription, which may seem to a logical mind totally incompatible with the heroes' behavior, is really a mark of the naïve, almost childlike quality of the Homeric world; and certainly human personality as such could not coexist with divine omnipotence. Yet the roots both of religious belief in the mastery of Zeus and of human pride in man's own abilities lay conjoined in the epics.

After the Homeric era men moved forward swiftly to command the foreground of Greek literature and art. Late Geometric potters enlarged their inherited stock of abstract motifs so as to give room to scenes of funerals (see Plate I), of battles by sea, or of horsemen with their great steeds (especially at Argos). In the Orientalizing wave of the seventh century men assumed fuller shape; gradually the animals and imaginary monsters which were initially popular slunk away, especially in Attic pottery. The first scene of epic or mythical context whose meaning we can certainly interpret is probably the battle of Heracles and the Amazon queen Andromeda on a clay disk from Tiryns about 700; but soon thereafter the blinding of Polyphemus appeared at Argos and Athens alike, and names such as Nessos or Menelaus were added to identify unmistakably the figures depicted. Large-scale sculpture, whether of human beings or of gods in human form, was under way by 650. Perhaps more significant as revelations of a sense of individual human significance are the signing of vases

[3] *Iliad* 1.218 (tr. Rouse). See generally the discussions in Fränkel, *DuP*; Jaeger, *Paideia*, I; Snell, *Discovery of the Mind*; Arthur W. H. Adkins, *Merit and Responsibility: A Study in Greek Values* (Oxford, 1960); and the works cited above, pp. 16–17, nn. 7–8.

and sculptures by their makers and the setting up of stone memorials:

> Let everyone, whether townsman or stranger from abroad, before he pass, mourn Tet[t]ichos, valorous man who died in battle and yielded up his tender youth: lamenting thus, proceed to worthy tasks.[4]

Such celebrations of the virtues of a dead man became fairly common by the sixth century.

Neither the exuberance of Orientalizing pottery nor the personal outpourings of loves and hates by the early lyric poets clearly manifest a decision by archaic Greeks to take command of their own lives. Unconsciously they did so; but on the conscious level they felt strongly the helplessness (*amechania*) of man in the turmoil of life.[5] The extraordinary degree to which their simple financial resources were lavished on temples and on dedicatory offerings in the sanctuary precincts manifests their deeply religious beliefs; even among the philosophers seeking to explain the nature of the universe in rational terms divine power remained strong. Thales is reputed to have said, "All is full of gods," a statement which, though apocryphal, represents an enduring, pantheistic aspect of Greek thought.[6]

One must therefore look beneath the surface to detect signs of a feeling that, while the gods in the end moved the world,

---

[4] Peek no. 1226; from the seventh century he has only Midas and one other (nos. 1413, 1171); those of the sixth century are more frequent, especially for men buried in an alien land (nos. 862, 75). Little detail appears until the fifth century (no. 417, after 472). On signatures see B. B. Shefton, *Journal of Hellenic Studies*, LXXXV (1965), p. 258; M. Guarducci, in G. M. A. Richter, *The Archaic Gravestones of Attica* (London, 1961), pp. 156–7.

[5] Rudolf Pfeiffer, "Gottheit und Individuum in der frühgriechischen Lyrik," *Philologus*, LXXXIV (1929), pp. 137–52; the term appears still in Simonides fr. 4 (to Scopas).

[6] Untersteiner, *Senofane*, pp. clxxvi–ix; W. Jaeger, *The Theology of the Early Greek Philosophers* (Oxford, 1947), on which cf. G. Vlastos, "Theology and Philosophy in Early Greek Thought," *Philosophical Quarterly*, II (1952), pp. 97–123.

men were *immediately* responsible for what occurred. A detailed exploration of this development, sure if concealed, would require extensive survey of many aspects of archaic civilization; one of these, the rise of concepts of natural causation through logical analysis, will be discussed in the next chapter. Other forces leading to the self-awareness of the individual man, however, can be noted briefly from the areas of political life and religious thought itself.

Inevitably the consolidation of the *polis* produced a feeling among its citizens and their leaders that their actions were significant. One student of Greek intellectual development goes so far as to argue that reason, in Hellas, was first expressed and formulated consciously on the political level, and certainly the ideal of the *polis* contained from the outset the implicit opinion that society could be improved through law.[7] Archilochus likened a city-state to a ship, and the metaphor that its leader was the steersman eventually became a commonplace. In Solon, collective responsibility for public action was a clearly enunciated principle; men might choose for themselves bad government or good (*eunomia*), and the poet himself could argue logically for the better course by pointing out the results which each would bring from the gods. Operating rationally on this basis, Solon even predicted the rise of the tyrant Pisistratus; and one provision of his laws had ordained that in public disputes every citizen must take a stand. The later reforms of Clisthenes, who reorganized the voting districts of Attica so as to break up old groupings, are a superb illustration of rational calculation in politics, resting fundamentally on the belief that the citizens of Attica did direct their destinies. When Herodotus later tapped men's memories as to the past of Athens, Sparta, Corinth, and other states, he

[7] Vernant, *Les Origines de la pensée grecque*, p. 127; Jaeger, *Paideia*, I, pp. 103–6. On Solon see frr. 10–11, and on *eunomia* fr. 3; cf. W. Jaeger, "Solons Eunomie," *SB Berlin Akademie* 1926, pp. 69–85; G. Vlastos, "Solonian Justice," *Classical Philology*, XLI (1946), pp. 65–83. Note also F. R. Adrados, "Origen del tema de la nave del estado en un papiro de Arquíloco," *Aegyptus*, XXXV (1955), pp. 206–10.

everywhere recounted the results in terms of leaders like Polycrates, Periander, Cleomenes, and a host of other major and minor figures.

In religious thought the human qualities of the gods bulked large from the days of Homer, but across the archaic era this view was markedly intensified. The rude figures of Geometric times, representing often generalized deities whom we can only call *Potnia theron* (Mistress of Animals) and the like, yielded to more sophisticated representations which archaeologists feel safe in labeling Artemis, Demeter, Athena, and so on; [8] statues of the major gods became ever more lifelike, in a human sense, as did their representations on vases (see Plate IIa).

At the same time the deities of Hellas, while still all-powerful, drew apart from the terrestrial sphere of human life and walked less often among men. The citizens of Athens could believe that the god Pan had appeared to the runner Philippides on his way to seek Spartan aid at the time of Marathon, and other evidence of direct divine intervention can be found in the fifth century; but divine retribution more often now operated through the actions of men themselves. Thus Aeschylus portrayed on his tragic stage human beings responsible for their actions. In sculpture, as in the Sunium relief of Plate IIb, one can sense the change as men "now begin to look inwards at themselves. And this new self-examination, though at first it evidently gives rise to thoughts of sombre tone, deepens the illusion that the statue is a person, a sentient being." [9]

While the cult of heroes, human beings of the past who were virtually or actually deified, stems from many sources, its rise across the archaic period may also be said to manifest an

[8] Starr, *Origins*, pp. 285–6.
[9] Bernard Ashmole, *The Classical Ideal in Greek Sculpture* (Semple Lectures, University of Cincinnati, 1964), p. 13; cf. Schefold, *Griechische Kunst als religiöses Phänomen*, pp. 76–7, 82, 85; Jaeger, *Paideia*, I, p. 227. On Aeschylus see Chapter VI.

increasing sense of human achievement. The valiant labors of
Heracles on man's behalf against a host of monsters were a
prime source for art and literature throughout the era; in the
sixth century Athens seized hold of and developed the story of
Theseus, the king who operated in a similar fashion in the
Saronic Gulf and also united and pacified Attica.[1] From this
reverence for mythical heroes it was no great step to Empedocles' praise of the historical character Pythagoras:

> There was living among them a man of surpassing knowl-
> edge, who had acquired the extremest wealth of the intellect,
> one expert in every kind of skilled activity. For whenever he
> reached out with his whole intellect, he easily discerned each
> one of existing things, in ten and even twenty lifetimes of
> mankind.[2]

By the fifth century men could be proud of the achievements of mankind, as we saw in Chapter III with respect to
the theory of progress. The physician Alcmaeon had drawn a
clear line between man and animals in his powers of comprehension; on the other end of the scale man had intruded some
distance on the erstwhile province of the gods. The great
change in this respect in the archaic era is obvious if one turns
directly from Homer to Pindar. For both the will of Zeus is
dominant, but the fifth-century poet speaks immediately of
men and treats them as self-moving.

That the intertwined factors noted in this chapter had a
direct bearing on the rise of a historical outlook is evident.
The *polis* became a conscious structure which produced
events (and records) of real significance for later generations
in its external wars and internal clashes; and the audience of
the city-state emerged into an active force, basically unified

[1] Thucydides 2.15.1–2; Plutarch, *Theseus;* Starr, *Origins,* pp. 287–91;
above p. 22, n. 6.
[2] Empedocles fr. 129. Fränkel, *DuP,* p. 327, finds in Ibycus 21 the first
praise of man's technical ability; Aristotle, *Rhetoric* 2.23.10 (1398b.10ff.),
cites from Alcidamas later examples of praise of wisdom.

while yet divided in various respects between commons and aristocrats—and these latter, in turn, all too prone to dissensions. To explain what had occurred in the past, as well as the course of the present, men now looked to themselves in the first instance, though always the gods loomed in the background. On the nature of man as then visualized, however, two significant qualifications are necessary if we are not unconsciously to apply modern views; both had important effects on the earliest historical writing.

In the first place, Greek thinkers did not jump from the concept that man moved himself to an idealization of mankind. Herodotus could be proud of the physical achievements of the tyrant Polycrates of Samos, whose great aqueduct tunnel is still one of the most impressive testimonials to the determination, daring, and skill of the sixth century; [3] but he used the whole record of Polycrates' tyranny as a warning against *hybris*. The ideas of *sophrosyne* and *hybris*, in truth, rose in prominence in the late archaic period as brakes on the unchaining of human action. Nor did men view the ordinary course of life as more than "petty, feeble, brief-lasting, and mingled with sorrows." [4] Greek historical thought, while savoring great deeds, was not likely to be imbued with facile optimism; its spirit was rather that of Pindar's magnificent outburst, the best single summation of archaic man's view of himself:

> Thing of a day! such is man; a shadow in a dream.
> Yet when god-given splendor visits him
> A bright radiance plays over him, and how sweet is life. [5]

Again, we must not ascribe to the archaic period, or to the fifth century either, a deep sense of individualism. Down to

[3] The most recent discussion is June Goodfield, "The Tunnel of Eupalinos," *Greek Heritage*, II, no. 6 (1965), pp. 66–74.
[4] Antiphon fr. 51 (Battegazzore and Untersteiner, *Sofisti*, IV, pp. 128–30); cf. J. C. Opstelten, *Sophocles and Greek Pessimism* (Amsterdam, 1952).
[5] Pindar, *Pyth.* 8.95–97, tr. H. D. F. Kitto, *The Greeks* (London, 1951), pp. 174–5.

400 B.C. the artistic representation of public figures remained a fascinating blend of typical and individual, as in the famous high-helmeted bust of Pericles. True individuation came only slowly in Greek art even in the fourth century; theoretical awareness of true personal differences scarcely appeared until the age of Alcibiades and Socrates, when exploration of ideas of man's nature (*physis*) became more extensive.[6] Not only was the art of biography absent until then, but also historical writing in its earliest stages could not possibly exhibit the sharp personalization of its characters which we expect today.

[6] Jaeger, *Paideia*, I, pp. 161–3; B. Snell, "Zur Soziologie des archaischen Griechentums: Der Einzelne und die Gruppe," *Gymnasium*, LXV (1958), pp. 48–58. The first authors to give really personal descriptions seem to have been Stesimbrotus and Ion (cf. H. Strasburger, *Festgabe für Paul Kirn* [Berlin, 1961], pp. 17–18).

CHAPTER 5

THE INTELLECTUAL DEVELOPMENT

OF THE SIXTH CENTURY

ᒣᒣᒣᒣᒣᒣᒣᒣᒣᒣᒣᒣᒣᒣᒣᒣᒣᒣᒣᒣᒣ

ONLY DURING the sixth century did the Greeks begin to think of space, time, man, and the state in any clear and coherent manner. At the threshold of the century stood Solon, amazingly advanced insofar as he deliberately assessed his own role and preached self-responsibility to his fellow Athenians; [1] yet it would be fair to say that neither he nor any of his contemporaries had a fully historical spirit. Politically their world had not yet entirely crystallized, nor did its activities offer men the long political memory they needed before they could look at the past historically. While human beings were growing more self-confident, Solon himself still placed the gods in very direct control of man and voiced the idea, "The mind of the Immortals is all unseen to man." More generally, intellectual analysis in Solon's day was still rudimentary, almost unconscious, and sporadic.

The emergence of a consecutive, connected chain of mental exploration was the prime contribution, intellectually considered, of the sixth and early fifth centuries. Across this period

[1] Gerald F. Else, *Origin and Early Forms of Greek Tragedy* (Cambridge, Mass., 1965), p. 42; Frederic Will, "Solon's Consciousness of Himself," *Transactions of the American Philological Association*, LXXXIX (1958), pp. 301–11. Mind of the Immortals: Solon fr. 17, cf. fr. 1.63ff.

thinker built upon thinker—and all upon the foundations of Homer and Hesiod, lyric and elegiac poets, and early religious speculation—to construct widely ranging, daring, yet logically based pictures of the world. Implicit in the evolution of disciplined thought during the sixth century were several qualities which must particularly interest anyone seeking the sources of the Greek historical attitude: its freedom of investigation, untrammeled by local or even Panhellenic patriotism or religious prescription; the effort to develop structures of causation in human terms; the rise of objectivity and impersonality, exhibited in satire and elsewhere; and, finally, the appearance of written prose as a vehicle for this analysis. These, in turn, rested upon deeper developments in men's perception of outside reality in connection with their own nature, developments which we can sense only partially in the shattered remains of sixth-century philosophy, art, and poetry.

The formal qualities just listed are often described in terms of the rise of philosophy. The appearance of this discipline was truly a great step; but to view the intellectual progress of the archaic period solely through philosophical spectacles is dangerously misleading and constricting. Beside the philosophers stood the contemporary poets and artists, who manifested much the same search and did so in a practical rather than theoretical context. Even in philosophy, we must remember, the distinction between abstract and concrete scarcely was felt until the days of Parmenides and later; and philosophic thinkers never lost complete sight of the ephemeral world about them in their search for unchanging verity.

The student of history, in particular, must not approach the sixth-century search for truth as an exclusively theoretical study; as will appear below, interest in specific facts of human existence, both past and present, also developed across the century until it produced the immediate forerunners of Herodotus, i.e., Hecataeus and the logographers. At that point we shall stand on the verge of the classic world of the fifth century, which made great leaps forward alike in arts, letters, and politics; but classic progress was possible only as a consequence of the achievements of the late archaic period.

THE RISE OF DISCIPLINED THOUGHT

Very early in the sixth century Thales of Miletus began talking, to those of his fellow citizens who were interested, about the origins of the physical world and probably about much else which is lost from our tradition. The ideas of Thales were in themselves not of great importance; what did matter was his effort to explain this development as a logical consequence of rational principles and also the fact that his public musings incited thinkers in a continuous chain. Across the sixth century Anaximander and then Anaximenes took giant intellectual strides in Ionia itself, where they were followed by Heraclitus early in the fifth century. Pythagoras and Xenophanes migrated to Italy and there spurred equally continuous speculation through the Pythagorean brotherhoods and the Eleatic school of Parmenides.

Ionia was the original center of consciously philosophical thought, but various parts of the Greek world had progressed to the point that they took fire from the first sparks. Nor was the rise of disciplined thought visible solely in philosophy. If one studies in detail the poets of the sixth century from Solon down through Theognis, Ibycus, and Simonides of Ceos, it is possible to detect, beneath poetic imagery, a parallel development of coherence in argument and analysis; and the famous series of male and female statues (*kouroi* and *korai*) carved by the sculptors of many regions display an almost consciously intellectual progress in analysis of the human form, encased though this vigorous geometry is in fundamentally abstract molds inherited from the seventh century. Even more obvious is the employment of rational calculation in political matters. Thales and Hecataeus both gave sober advice to their fellow

Ionians faced by outside threats, while Clisthenes shrewdly rearranged the Athenian polity.[2]

To survey the course of philosophy, poetry, and art across the sixth century would immerse us in a great sea of detail, which has often been surveyed in recent years; the important matter for our purposes is the evolution of intellectual attitudes essential for the eventual appearance of an audience which could appreciate and support a historical outlook. Always, however, one must keep in mind the simple background out of which conscious analysis arose, in order to appreciate the magnitude of the progress. As Guthrie has well said, with respect to philosophy,

> The Milesians had no philosophical predecessors. Before they embarked on their conscious reflective activity, the ideas which filled their heads concerning the nature and working of the universe were derived from popular pre-philosophical thought, steeped in myth, and it is perhaps worth noting that the only literature with which they were acquainted was poetical. Moreover the bonds of language, in which all philosophy is to a greater or less degree enmeshed, lay particularly heavy upon them, for they had not the latter-day advantage of reading in a variety of tongues. The degree to which they attained a rational outlook is admittedly astonishing. The mere fact of writing in prose was a great step forward.[3]

On the philosophic and scientific side advance was based upon the firm belief that the world could best be understood and explained by rational, organized, and consecutive thought. Reason early became an independent quality in the Greek world, as distinct from matter,[4] though one must doubt that its followers in the sixth century were altogether consciously aware that they were being "rational." By the fifth century logic and geometry were elaborated as conscious tools

[2] Herodotus 1.75, 170 (Thales); 5.36, 125 (Hecataeus); Lévêque and Vidal-Naquet, *Clisthène*, pp. 66–8.
[3] Guthrie, *Greek Philosophy*, I, p. 118.
[4] Fränkel, *DuP*, p. 86, n. 10.

of analysis, but this development does not directly concern us; historians have rarely made serious use of syllogisms or geometric proofs. A number of attendant developments, however, must excite one's interest.

First of all, the freedom of thought of the age is remarkable. While each of the philosophers might pontifically assert that he alone had discovered basic reality, his ideas were brought to light only to face ruthless criticism in the market place. The intellectual freedom with which thinkers—and poets and artists as well—pursued their explorations was an inheritance from the open and self-expressive character of seventh-century aristocratic society, as exhibited in the forceful poems of Archilochus and Alcaeus, but it was intensified and structured by the men of the sixth century. That "curiosity" which is so often singled out as one of Herodotus' principal drives was not really a naïve quality but the fruit of an open, active mind relatively untrammeled by religious and political prescription.

Another significant quality of sixth-century thought was its effort to establish natural causes and laws for terrestrial phenomena. The distinction between cause and matter remained shadowy down to Empedocles, but all good cosmogonists searched for an *aitia* or original source. The one surviving fragment of Anaximander's works, quoted in Chapter III above, insists that the physical world contains regular payment of penalty and retribution for injustice; and from the time of Solon's famous statement,

> The strength of snow and of hail is from a cloud, and thunder comes from the bright lightning; a city is destroyed by great men, and the common folk fall into bondage to a despot because of ignorance

the concept of natural cause and effect was applied to human society as well.[5] In the fifth century an excellent example is

[5] Solon frr. 8, 10; in fr. 3 the effects of good and ill are graphically described in one of our earliest connected analyses. *Aitia:* Guthrie, *Greek Philosophy,* I, p. 6; II, p. 159; Jaeger, *Paideia,* I, p. 220.

the effort of *On Airs Waters Places* to explain divergences among peoples on the basis of climate, topography, and other natural factors.

On the theory of natural causation, nevertheless, qualification is immediately in order, especially if one is to understand Herodotus and his audience. The triumph of rationality did not extend beyond the most advanced circles, and even there did not sweep away the power of the gods, as I noted at the close of the preceding chapter. "In all early philosophical literature," di Santillana observes, "understanding and the Way of the Gods are one," a statement which could be applied to sixth-century culture generally.[6] What was grasped at this time, especially by Xenophanes, was that the gods were of a different order from men and also that the human universe was to be understood first on a natural level. Later on, the divine will stood over all earthly happenings in Herodotus' history no less than it did in the Homeric epics; still, Herodotus clearly felt that his great tale made sense in earthly terms. In this respect the limited role of natural principles in his work perhaps helped lead Herodotus to emphasize the rich diversity and unpredictability of human beings, matters which Thucydides had also to admit but found far harder to justify within his pattern of laws of human behavior.

A third attribute of sixth-century culture, which is not as often noticed as it deserves to be, was an incipient tendency for authors to treat the world about them and their own role therein with impersonal objectivity. Homer had possessed this quality in an undeveloped manner, but in the lyric outburst and political passion of the seventh century it temporarily vanished. Philosophers too had their overweening pride, which extended beyond their theoretical analyses; Heraclitus, no less than the poet Archilochus, expressed strong personal views on the political events of his native city.[7]

[6] G. di Santillana, *Prologue to Parmenides* (Semple Lectures, University of Cincinnati, 1964), p. 6.
[7] Heraclitus frr. 44, 104, 121.

Here and there, however, the lyric discovery of the self led men like Solon to look at themselves objectively, and in such poetry as Alcman's choral lyrics for the maids of Sparta the work was distinguished from the person of the poet. As time went on, some men came to view the world about them coolly. The ties of local partiality were weakened among those poets and thinkers who migrated in the upheavals of the era, as did Herodotus later; it is also worth noting that humor and satire evolved above the naïve level expressed in the *Homeric Hymn to Hermes* and other early works. Hipponax of Ephesus, about 510, was famous for his bitter caricatures and grotesques, by which he deliberately sought to entertain his audience and in which he temporarily assumed a role.[8] In the same period a few vases were decorated with intentionally humorous scenes,[9] and the poet Anacreon showed a gift for irony, a spirit which could maintain its "distance from its subjects and so from itself" so that each hearer could interpret Anacreon's works for himself. Despite the mercurial character of the Greeks as citizens and as thinkers this ability to assess life dispassionately was to become a significant element in classic art and tragedy; especially for history it was essential. For always the historian must be able "to get outside himself in some fashion," i.e., to look at the past for itself.[1]

[8] Fränkel, *DuP*, pp. 246–9; Olivier Masson, *Les Fragments du poète Hipponax* (Paris, 1962); cf. W. Binsfeld, *Grylloi: Ein Beitrag zur Geschichte der antiken Karikatur* (Diss. Köln, 1956). Probably the *Batrachomyomachia* and *Margites* are as early or earlier than Hipponax; Simonides seems to jest in fr. 23 (520 B.C.) and fr. 22.
[9] Thus an amphora by Amasis, showing satyrs making wine, in Würzburg (E. Langlotz, *Griechische Vasen in Würzburg* [Munich, 1932], no. 265, pl. 73–4). The burlesque Boeotian black-figure vases found at the shrine of the Kabirion are of the late fifth (or even fourth) century; cf. Paul Wolters, *Das Kabirenheiligtum bei Theben*, I (Berlin, 1940); Peter Levi, "A Kabirion Vase," *Journal of Hellenic Studies*, LXXXIV (1964), pp. 155–6.
[1] I. Meyerson, *Journal de psychologie*, LIII (1956), p. 336; Hermann Strasburger, "Komik und Satire in der griechischen Geschichtsschreibung," *Festgabe für Paul Kirn* (Berlin, 1961), pp. 13–45, shows that these qualities were not favored until the fourth century and thereafter. Anacreon: Fränkel, *DuP*, pp. 334, 342.

If men were to express their thoughts in a more connected and logical fashion than had ever before been necessary, they also required a developed mode of communication; for though even philosophers spoke in the first instance, they also wrote down their ideas at least from Anaximander onward. This need, while felt in the sixth century, was only partially satisfied at the time, either in the arts or in literature—it is not solely because our knowledge rests on fragments that we often fail to understand clearly the meaning of a philosopher or poet of the period. Stesichorus and Ibycus nonetheless took great steps toward elaborating a narrative style which organized events rather than putting them simply one after another. In Anacreon's poetry each element appeared at the point where classic order would marshal it; and such a sculptured group as the battle between gods and giants on the Siphnian frieze (Plate VIIa) interrelated figures in what may be termed a narrative approach.[2]

One consequence was the elevation of prose from the primitive level of early treaties and laws to an artistic medium. The first prose writer was said to be Pherecydes of Syros about the midpoint of the sixth century; but Anaximander, Alcmaeon, Hecataeus, and the logographers all turned to prose as more suitable for their thoughts than was the necessarily personal and immediate medium of poetry. Herodotus' style was directly descended from archaic modes of composition, rich in digressions which weakened the dominance of guiding concepts, not always clear in transitions, often abrupt in conclusion.[3] While these traits may occasionally confuse a reader of the first Greek history, we must be grateful that in his apparently coursing, yet actually elaborated narrative Herodotus

[2] C. Picard and P. de la Coste-Messelière, *Fouilles de Delphes*, IV.2 (Paris, 1928), pp. 72ff., c.525 B.C. Cf. Fränkel, *DuP*, pp. 321, 325, 335.
[3] B. A. van Groningen, *La composition littéraire archaïque grecque* (2d ed.; Groningen, 1960); see earlier W. Aly, *Formprobleme der frühen griechischen Prosa* (Leipzig, 1929). Pherecydes: Fränkel, *DuP*, pp. 280–2; F. Jacoby, *Abhandlungen zur griechischen Geschichtschreibung* (Leiden, 1956), pp. 106–9.

could avoid the imagery which makes Parmenides so difficult or the reiterated interweaving of argument which marks Empedocles' work.

THE ROAD OF SPECULATIVE REASON

Among the criteria for judging a historical account truth stands sovereign today. History is not alone in this respect; virtually all modern intellectual studies require truth in the sense of accurate, precise information. Many men of the sixth century B.C. also seem to have been seeking the truth (*aletheia*), but if we are to understand their search we must not import our own, developed concepts too far into the archaic world.[4] What they meant by truth did not entirely agree with our definition; above all, the methods by which they expected to establish it differed radically from those of modern times.

Since these points have a very direct relevance to the rise of history and also help to account for some of its early characteristics, one must regret that the evidence for the archaic connotations of truth has never been fully and rigorously analyzed. Perhaps the matter has appeared simple, but the common tendency to interpret the sixth-century drive for truth solely in terms of an abstract, theoretical study leads to misunderstandings from the outset.

Homer knew words for "false" and "true," but such terms suggested only a very rudimentary, though genuine, distinction between true and untrue. Deliberate lies were generally abhorrent, a trick for women and alien to the warrior's code, though useful deceit had its place especially in the *Odyssey*. Theoretical distinction between "lie" and "error" did not yet appear in the word *pseudos*; nor, on the other side, did terms such as *atrekes*, *eteos*, or *etumos* make any distinction between

[4] The point is stressed by W. Luther, "Der frühgriechische Wahrheitsgedanke im Lichte der Sprache," *Gymnasium*, LXV (1958), pp. 75–107.

"actual situations" and "truth." The word most commonly used for "true" in later Greek, *alethes*, was employed by Homer almost exclusively with verbs of saying as an object, not an adverbial modifier, to connote "precision and clarity."[5] The lack of any clear method for establishing genuine truth shows perhaps most clearly in the manner in which Alcinous decided that Odysseus was not a fashioner of lies but had told a true tale: "Upon thee is grace of words, and within thee is a heart of wisdom, and thy tale thou hast told with skill, as doth a minstrel."[6]

Already in the *Odyssey*, as compared with the *Iliad*, hints of the distinction between true and false deepened. Hesiod separated the two further in his poetic effort to lead men on the right path. At the outset of the *Works and Days* he promised to tell *etetuma*—"reality" perhaps, but also with a flavor of "truth"—and in the *Theogony* the Muses made the significant assertion that "we know how to speak many false things as though they were true; but we know, when we will, to utter true things." Not until the time of Solon, however, can we clearly see in the surviving literature that the ideal of truth had begun to rise to the status of an abstract virtue.[7] From this point on the search for truth slowly became more deliberate and conscious both in literature and in art.

The direction taken by the philosophic seekers was significantly influenced by the lack of an inherited abstract concept

[5] Accame, *Rivista di filologia*, XCII (1964), p. 264; Luther, *"Wahrheit" und "Lüge" im ältesten Griechentum;* Otfrid Becker, *Das Bild des Weges und verwandte Vorstellungen im frühgriechischen Denken, Hermes,* Einzelschrift IV (Berlin, 1937), pp. 105–10; R. Maschke, *Die Willenslehre im griechischen Recht* (Berlin, 1926); Louis Gernet, *Recherches sur le développement de la pensée juridique et morale en Grèce* (Paris, 1917), pp. 350–88.
[6] *Odyssey* 11.367–8.
[7] Hesiod: Luther, *Wahrheit,* pp. 20–3; Jaeger, *Paideia,* I, p. 112. Solon frr. 9, 11, 24; fr. 21 proclaims, "Poets tell many lies." In Mimnermus fr. 8 truth is hailed as "the most righteous of all things." See Heinimann, *Nomos und Physis,* pp. 43–58; S. Accame, "L'Ispirazione della musa e gli albori della critica storica nell'età arcaica," *Rivista di filologia,* XCII (1964), pp. 129–56, 257–87.

of truth and also by the uneasy doubt, common to all thinkers in early Greek civilization, that men could not know the truth unless the gods vouchsafed them knowledge. Homer and Hesiod thus appealed to a goddess or to the Muses to let them tell their tales, and the opposition between divine certainty and human ignorance became a poetic commonplace. Xenophanes went on to generalize this attitude in a fascinating statement,

> As for certain truth, no man has seen it, nor will there ever be a man who knows about the gods and above all the things I mention. For if he succeeds to the full in saying what is completely true, he himself is nevertheless unaware of it; and Opinion (*dokos*) is fixed by fate upon all things.[8]

In the next century the sophists were partly indifferent to the question whether one could establish truth or, in the case of Gorgias, could construct an ironic argument that even if anything existed, we could not know it; nor, should we know, could we communicate our knowledge.[9]

To the historical effects of this sense of mortal fallibility I shall return in a moment. In practice the Greek thinkers who lived amidst the expanding, if unstable society of the sixth and fifth centuries could not endure an attitude of complete intellectual doubt; whether philosopher, poet, or historian, they often proclaimed that they were telling the truth.[1] How, in human terms, could they justify their assertions?

Here the road eventually bifurcated; and of the two

[8] Xenophanes fr. 35. Guthrie, *Greek Philosophy*, I, pp. 395–99, has further references to Heraclitus, Parmenides, Empedocles, Democritus, and Herodotus (7.50.2); see also Snell, *Discovery of the Mind*, pp. 136–52; Guthrie, *Twentieth Century Approaches to Plato* (Semple Lectures, University of Cincinnati, 1963). Theognis 141–2 sums up the view: "We men practise vain things, knowing naught, while the Gods accomplish all to their mind."

[9] Guthrie, *Greek Philosophy*, II, p. 17. Antiphon, however, wrote a book on Truth, apparently dealing with the theory of knowledge (Battegazzore and Untersteiner, *Sofisti*, IV, pp. 4–5, 34ff.).

[1] Luther, *Wahrheit*, pp. 126–7, draws up a list of such protestations.

approaches—speculative reason and factual observation (*historie*)—the former was ever more favored by philosophic thinkers. Men of this persuasion increasingly tended to deny or to discount the evidence of the physical senses as a base for truth and instead to trust in reason alone.[2] In doing so the philosophers could rely upon an innate Greek feeling that one could "know" (*noein*) by some mode of perception independent of the senses; as Aristotle later summed up this view, "of the thinking states by which we grasp truth, some are unfailingly true, others admit of error—opinion, for instance, and calculation, whereas scientific knowing and intuition are always true." Much earlier Heraclitus had drawn a clear line between the product of mental speculation and the purported knowledge born of factual study:

> Much learning (*polymathie*) does not teach one to have intelligence; for it would have taught Hesiod and Pythagoras, and again, Xenophanes and Hecataeus.[3]

Heraclitus himself paraded divine inspiration; his virtual contemporary Parmenides placed his revelation of the way of truth in the mouth of the goddess Aletheia herself. Both used also theoretical tools, especially those of logic, to support their arguments, and the Pythagoreans employed geometry, at once precise in method and abstract in its drive toward generalization.

Although the philosophers were not as dominant in Greek thought as modern studies of Hellenic culture often suggest, the increasing emphasis on speculative reason intensified, as

---

[2] The goddess Aletheia had already warned Parmenides (fr. 1.30) that in the world of the senses there was "no true belief (ταῖς οὐκ ἔνι πίστις ἀληθής)."

[3] Heraclitus fr. 40; cf. frr. 28, 78, 79, 83, 102; cf. Untersteiner, *Senofane*, pp. 17–18. *Nous:* Aristotle, *Posterior Analytics* 2.19 (100b.5–9, tr. Mure); Guthrie, *Greek Philosophy*, II, pp. 17–19; Kurt von Fritz, "ΝΟΥΣ, NOEIN and their Derivatives in pre-Socratic Philosophy (excluding Anaxagoras)," *Classical Philology*, XL (1955), pp. 223–42; XLI (1946), pp. 12–34; B. Snell, *Die Ausdrücke für den Begriff des Wissens in der vorplatonischen Philosophie* (Berlin, 1924).

well as reflected, a fundamental characteristic of Greek civilization. Men of this stamp seem often to have been as bent upon constructing logically coherent structures within the framework of inherited concepts as upon establishing demonstrable verity; so too artists of the sixth century sought to depict the muscles and form of the human body only within the abstract schemata of archaic sculpture. Truth, in other words, was a matter of internal consistency insofar as men could hope to establish it.

The bearing of this attitude for history was of importance. If Herodotus only very rarely asserted that something was genuinely true, his reserve was in part a purely historical caution, born of a proper suspicion of the reliability of oral sources; but we must also keep in mind the general doubt whether truth was entirely ascertainable by human means. Later historians, strongly under the influence of literary style and rhetorical development, could not consciously oppose the resulting tendencies which impelled them toward distortion; for truth, while dimly felt to be significant, was not a fetish.[4] Iron insistence upon the specifically accurate, whether in numbers, quotations, or other respects, is a very recent attribute of historical and scholarly work in general. Its complement, the distinction of "certain," "probable," and merely "possible," could appear only sporadically in early Greek thought.[5]

THE ROAD OF FACTUAL RESEARCH

Yet history did eventually become a conscious intellectual discipline, and its first practitioner, Herodotus, surely felt that

[4] Herman Peter, *Wahrheit und Kunst: Geschichtsschreibung und Plagiat im klassischen Altertums* (Leipzig, 1911), ch. i; U. von Wilamowitz-Moellendorff, *Greek Historical Writing* (Oxford, 1908).
[5] Xenophanes fr. 35 seems to contain the first clear assertion of something as "probable" (Fränkel, *DuP*, p. 383; Guthrie, *Greek Philosophy*, I, p. 396).

what he had to say was not only amusing, not only elevating, but also fundamentally true, even though his story rested on quite another base than that of speculative reason. We must not be mislead into sundering the theoretical approach, as if it were the realm of true seekers after wisdom in early Greece, from the world of *historie,* or "factual research." Distinction between matter and spirit was still rudimentary in Empedocles, the earliest to draw a real line in this respect; Parmenides, in the previous generation, may be termed the first metaphysician, but still he devoted very serious consideration to the realm of *doxa,* which in his poem seems to embrace the physical firmament and earth.⁶ Earlier, Xenophanes, while skeptical of man's ability to know matters divine, trusted empirical observation for earthly affairs; criticized by Heraclitus for his *polymathie* as a result, he drew lessons from fossils and is reported to have written on the foundation of Colophon and colonization of Elea.

These early thinkers, after all, did not possess the rigorous discipline of modern philosophy; nor did they fully abandon factual information in favor of abstract reasoning. Pythagoras had practical skills and developed his theories of harmonics from a specific observation; Anaximander, it is claimed, described the actual world; other philosophers are known to have suggested experiments to prove their points.⁷ In philosophical theories of the sixth and fifth centuries the views of heavenly bodies, of earth, of animals, and of man's own physical nature developed as much toward "reality" as did the

⁶ Di Santillana, *Prologue to Parmenides:* Hans Schwabl, "Sein und Doxa bei Parmenides," *Wiener Studien,* LXVI (1953), pp. 50–75. Xenophanes: Diogenes Laertius 9.20; Lesky, *History of Greek Literature,* p. 208; Guthrie, *Greek Philosophy,* I, p. 365; Untersteiner, *Senofane,* pp. ccl–iv. The existence of his historical poems is simply denied by Jacoby, *Abhandlungen,* p. 149 n. 27. On Xenophanes' distinction of divine and earthly affairs, cf. Luther, *Gymnasium,* LXV (1958), pp. 82–3; Fränkel, *DuP,* p. 387.
⁷ Guthrie, *Greek Philosophy,* I, pp. 173–7; on Anaximander, see Chapter II above. Experiment: Plutarch, *Moralia* 947F; B. Farrington, *Greek Science,* I (Harmondsworth, 1944), pp. 34, 47, 55–6, 59.

corresponding artistic shift from archaic to classical styles. A recent critic has justly observed that one finds always in Greek philosophy an effort "to move back to a view of reality compatible with what men directly experience. This common-sense resilience is an important part of what is often mentioned but seldom examined, the clarity of Greek thought." [8]

If some thinkers reached for the invisible laws of the universe with their feet firmly on this earth, most men must have remained totally earth-bound. Greek society, after all, was insistent upon enjoying, as much as human frailty and sorrows permitted, the sunlight of life. Craftsmen, who worked with the real, always enjoyed honorable respect; in the sixth century especially there came a great outburst of construction of temples, walls, harbors, and other works to manifest man's ability at enlarging and consolidating his framework of existence. It is small wonder if even philosophers like Pythagoras and Xenophanes clung to the *polymathie* which Heraclitus condemned, and so broadened out the path of scientific inquiry (the *doxa* of Pythagorean thought) or of research (the *historie* of Herodotus). The travelers on this road, while aware sometimes of the fallibility of the senses, nonetheless clung to observation and recording of specific fact. This approach, too, was deeply rooted in the past; for poets from Homer on dealt always "with fact, or what is believed to be fact, and never with fiction." [9]

The most deliberate defense of factual investigation appeared in the rise of scientific medicine. The first great doctor was that fascinating figure, Alcmaeon of Croton (*c.*480–40), who left certainty to the gods; "men can only follow the signs given to them in the visible world and by interpreting them feel their way towards the unseen." [1] Thence sprang the em-

---

[8] G. S. Kirk, "Sense and Common-sense in the Development of Greek Philosophy," *Journal of Hellenic Studies*, LXXXI (1961), pp. 105–17, on p. 117.
[9] Selincourt, *World of Herodotus*, p. 284; cf. Fränkel, *DuP*, pp. 293–5.
[1] Alcmaeon fr. 1, as interpreted by Guthrie, *Greek Philosophy*, I, p. 344.

pirical attitude which later led to the composition of the important Hippocratic essay *On Ancient Medicine*. The argument of this work, written in the latter part of the fifth century, is a rebuttal of theoretical analysis which claims to know the truth, but does not; for its followers hold no method by which to establish verities.[2] Only by "precise" observation and "sensibility of the body" can the medical man hope to gain true knowledge. This essay is the most direct justification of a reliance on "fact" of which we know down to 400.

Others followed the same method in a less conscious fashion; and among these figures the logographers and Hecataeus must especially command our attention. These predecessors of Herodotus throw considerable light upon his choice of subject matter and method of approach, as well as illustrating the increasingly clear view of space and time which obtained at the close of the archaic period.

Hecataeus (*c.*560–480) is the most considerable of these forerunners and has often been presented as the intellectual mentor of Herodotus.[3] To explain the rise of history by throwing it back from the first known historian to a more shadowy figure in the preceding generation is a rather naïve procedure; and in any case there must be considerable doubt whether Hecataeus can in any serious sense be called a historian. His *Periegesis* was clearly a geographical and partly anthropological survey of the coasts of the Mediterranean and some inland districts; in this treatise there does appear a clear sense of space and also at various points a concept that the past had been a long period of time in which change occurred.[4] His

[2] *On Ancient Medicine* 36 (ed. Heiberg): οὐ γάρ ἐστι πρὸς ὅ τι χρή ἀνενέγκαντα εἰδέναι τὸ σάφες; on precision, cc. 41, 44, with Luther, *Gymnasium*, LXV (1958), p. 104.
[3] F. Jacoby, *Griechische Historiker* (Stuttgart, 1956), and *Abhandlungen*, pp. 20, 77ff.; G. de Sanctis, "Intorno al razionalismo di Ecateo," *Studi di storia della storiografia greca* (Florence, 1951), pp. 3–19. But see Momigliano, *Studies in Historiography*, p. 211; L. Pearson, *Early Ionian Historians* (Oxford, 1939), p. 27.
[4] Cf. Herodotus 2.143 on Hecataeus' counting of generations, and Hecataeus frr. 130, 138, 288, 388 (Nenci); see W. von Leyden, "Spatium

other work, *Genealogiae*, seems to have been nothing more than a rationalization of Hellenic myths; its opening remark was probably the statement, "I write the following as it seems to me to be true; for the *logoi* of the Greeks are many and, as it seems to me, foolish."

Although this has often been seized upon as representing a truly historical, critical approach, more probably Hecataeus was asserting simply that the *logoi* were foolish only because contradictory.[5] Certainly his arbitrary reconstructions on the basis of myth were subject to criticism in later times, once historical standards had really appeared. From the relatively few surviving fragments of the second work his approach seems to have been more learned than critical; of truly historical material there is no evidence. Hecataeus' value for later development lies principally in his insistence on recording his observation of physical reality in the *Periegesis* and in his example to Herodotus of "research" (*historie*) which sought to write "as it seems to me to be true (ὥς μοι δοκεῖ ἀληθέα εἶναι)."

As for the early Ionian logographers such as Xanthus of Lydia, who is said to have given the "starting point" to Herodotus, almost no fragments survive; and dating is more than obscure.[6] Our most extensive discussion, by Dionysius of Halicarnassus in the late first century B.C., asserts that they

---

Historicum," *Durham University Journal*, n.s. XI (1950), pp. 89–104. It deserves notice, however, that the word *chronos* does not appear at all in surviving fragments.

[5] This introduction is commonly assigned to the *Genealogiae*, as by Jacoby, *FGrH*, no. 1, F 1a; but others place it at the beginning of the *Periegesis*. Pearson, *Early Ionian Historians*, pp. 97–8, feels it could have been in either work. Nenci, *Hecataei Milesii Fragmenta*, pp. xxiii–vi, advances the view given in the text and points out that if Hecataeus had disbelieved the myths he would not have manipulated them by means of etymological criticism and other techniques.

[6] Pearson, *Early Ionian Historians*, and *The Local Historians of Attica* (Lancaster, Pa., 1942). Xanthus the "starting point" for Herodotus: Ephorus in Athenaeus 12.515e, with the discussion in Pearson, *Early Ionian Historians*, pp. 109ff. J. M. Stahl, "Über den Zusammenhang der ältesten griechischen Geschichtschreibung mit der epischen Dichtung," *Neue Jahrbücher für Philologie und Paedagogik*, CLIII (1896), pp. 369–78, still has value.

dealt with "individual peoples and cities separately" with the object of bringing to light "the written records that they found preserved in temples or in secular buildings in the form in which they found them" and in a style "clear, simple, unaffected, and concise."

The report of Dionysius has been seriously attacked both on the grounds that interest in records per se is a more Hellenistic than Hellenic attitude and, more generally, on the principle that interest in the history of specific cities emerged only in the latter part of the fifth century as a compensation for the failure of general Hellenic histories to treat adequately of local glories.[7] The latter argument, most forcefully advanced by Jacoby, smacks of the theoretical, though one may agree that our evidence does show a great development of local history in the fourth century and in the subsequent Hellenistic era. Either Dionysius or his sources could have read the work of many men who are only names to us, and it seems unreasonable to deny that the burgeoning intellectual activity of the archaic era could have produced some sort of semihistorical accounts in prose as well as the epics of the Homeric and Theban cycles, the narrative dithyrambs of Stesichorus and other poets, and the genealogical poetry of men like Panyassis (d. 460 B.C.), uncle of Herodotus.[8] In the absence of adequate bodies of fragments we cannot tell to what extent such prose works were genuinely historical; the term *logos*, almost untranslatable, meant at this time "a description which at the same time explains."[9]

[7] Dionysius of Halicarnassus, *de Thucydide* 5 (tr. Pearson, *Early Ionian Historians*, pp. 3–4); Truesdell Brown, *American Historical Review*, LIX (1954), pp. 834–8; F. Jacoby, *Atthis* (Oxford, 1949), pp. 199–201, in PW *s.v.* Herodotos, cols. 354–5, and *FGrH* 3.b, Suppl. I (1954). U. von Wilamowitz-Moellendorff, *Aristoteles und Athen* (Berlin, 1893), I, pp. 277ff., II, pp. 17ff., supports the idea of early local history. See also Strasburger, *Saeculum*, V (1954), pp. 397–8.
[8] Panyassis also wrote an *Ionica* on the foundation of the Ionian states; see F. Stoessl in PW *s.v.* Panyassis. Note too Acusilaus of Argos, about 500 B.C., who turned epic into prose (a fragment in *Ox. Pap.* XIII.1611 = *FGrH*, no. 2, F 22).
[9] Guthrie, *Greek Philosophy*, I, p. 38; cf. Pearson, *Early Ionian Historians*, p. 5.

The important aspect of the logographers is the fact that they did describe earthly events in the belief, we must assume, that this description had value. In this respect they clung to the world of *doxa*, and as Alcmaeon led on to scientific medicine so these dim figures led on to the work of Herodotus. While the first historian never directly argued for the superiority of his method over the speculative approach, as does the author of *On Ancient Medicine*, one can see in his comments on Hecataeus' map a disdain for the purely theoretical.[1] The rise of history, in sum, owes much to the systematic, critical, and objective standards developed by sixth-century thinkers, but its origins can never be explained by reference to that speculative attitude which was represented by the main drive of philosophic meditation; its roots lie rather in the companion path, that of factual recountal and analysis.

THE ARCHAIC AGE

The achievements of archaic civilization, 700–500 B.C., are many and marvelous. Summing them up as a base for the subsequent evolution of Greek civilization rather than in their own right, one may note the consolidation of political units both geographically and spiritually; the rise of an alert citizenry which formed an ever more conscious audience alike in political and in cultural matters; the crystallization of artistic and literary forms; and the appearance of conscious intellectual procedures for exploring man and the world about him.

So great was the progress that the observer may be bemused into overlooking the incoherencies and weaknesses still evident—again measuring from what was to come thereafter in the classic era. History could not have been written in the age of Solon; nor, as far as we can see, does it seem to have appeared at the close of the sixth century. Only by the end of

---

[1] Herodotus 4.36; cf. Jaeger, *Paideia*, I, pp. 214–15.

the archaic age was space a precise concept, especially in the aspect of clear awareness of differences among Mediterranean societies. A theory of time, as a chronological structure in which change could be apprehended, developed with equal slowness. Sharpness of intellectual analysis, as we have observed in this chapter, scarcely emerged before the sixth century, and one of the major roads toward truth tended strongly to lead its followers away from any possible historical interest.

To conclude this survey of archaic civilization, let us turn to its vases, for these suggest in visual form its major qualities. One of the most delightful products of later sixth-century Attic workshops is the cup by Exekias shown on Plate IIa. Here Dionysus sails across a dolphin-studded sea, an imaginary world far removed from the realities of the faction-ridden Attica of the time. The scene is animated by an engaging exuberance which at first sight may seem naïve, but on closer inspection this vigor clearly appears to be harnessed in skillfully elaborated forms. The same characteristics mark the literature of the era. Dominated by personal emotion and curiosity, archaic authors were spurred to pile up detail and to pour forth a rich succession of ideas almost—but not quite—pell-mell.

These latter attributes show clearly on the famous François crater, where band after band of amazingly complicated decoration proffer more than two hundred figures of gods and men in scenes which have some sense of narration even though they jump from one mythical event to another.[2] Or, again, take vases which have independent decoration on their two major sides. Such scenes may be connected or, while drawn from different mythical cycles, may suggest the same kind of battle or event or may have absolutely no connection in theme or spirit.[3] Of historical scenes there is little trace; the one sure

[2] Schefold, *Sagenbilder,* pp. 54–5, 60, 86.
[3] E.g., a Duris cup c.490, *CVA* Austria 1, pl. 11–12 (Wien 1), Inv. 3695, shows connected scenes relating to the contention over the arms of Achilles; so too the deeds of Theseus in *CVA* Italy 30, pl. 1343 (Florence

example before 500 B.C. is the Arcesilaus cup (Plate III), of Laconian origin and presumably representing a king of Cyrene.[4] Even so the student interested in the rise of a truly historical spirit will find food for thought in sixth-century vases by reason of their specific identification of epic characters, their emphasis on human scenes, and their suggestion that the events portrayed are important.

Neither the style of archaic vases nor, for that matter, the techniques of contemporary literary composition show qualities which a modern historian will easily comprehend; the inheritance of the archaic age was not consciously historical. The last great literary figure before 500, Theognis, disliked the present and looked to the past, when the "good men" or born aristocrats held full sway; but his bitter elegiac exhortations to Cyrnus contain no attempt whatever to re-create that past as a historic period. Nevertheless, as the preceding chapters have sought to demonstrate, theme by theme, the attitudes necessary to produce an audience willing to listen to history had now emerged. Their fruition came in the next century as the vigorous activity of the classic era threw up a host of specialized literary and intellectual approaches to the study of man.

---

3), Inv. 91456, a cup c.510. For examples of scenes from different cycles but similar in spirit, cf. *CVA* Deutschland 22, pl. 1043 (Berlin 3), F 2538, hunts; *CVA* Greece 1, pl. 26 (Athens 1), Inv. 1666, heroes against human opponents; *CVA* Italy 36, pl. 1618 (Capitoline Museum 1), no. 47, heroes against animals.
[4] On this much debated vase, see recently S. Benton, *Archaeology*, XII (1959), pp. 178ff.; Arias-Hirmer, *Tausend Jahre griechische Vasenkunst*, on pl. 74. In Ionian black-figure king Cambyses *may* appear on a fragment from Old Smyrna about 520–10 B.C. (J. M. Cook, *Annual of the British School at Athens*, LX [1965], pp. 136–7).

CHAPTER 6

THE APPEARANCE

OF HISTORY

ᒐᒐᒐᒐᒐᒐᒐᒐᒐᒐᒐᒐᒐᒐᒐᒐᒐᒐᒐᒐᒐᒐ

THE FIRST GREAT HISTORY, which dealt with the Persian Wars through 479 B.C., was written at Athens, the home of tragedy. Its author was an exile from Halicarnassus, Herodotus, who was educated in Ionian rationalism and also steeped in the epic tradition. These facts I stress deliberately, for at one time or another each has been advanced as a sufficient cause for the appearance of history.

As attendant circumstances they certainly influenced the manner in which Herodotus marshaled his history; but if the argument of the preceding chapters has any validity we cannot look to such contemporary, external conditions to find the fundamental forces which led either Herodotus or his audience to think historically. Herodotus, after all, tells us why he wrote—"in the hope of thereby preserving from decay the remembrance of what men have done, and of preventing the great and wonderful actions of the Greeks and Barbarians from losing their due meed of glory; and withal to put on record what were their grounds of feud." The tale was to be one of great deeds, as were the Homeric epics, but it would be a reasoned account of the past sensed as past, the truth of which Herodotus felt he could assess. In short, it was to be history.

The appearance of this work in the fifth century represents the sum or amalgamation of those views of space, time, state, and mankind which had been evolving across the archaic age. Undoubtedly the Persian Wars served admirably as a precipitating catalyst; for this outside intrusion into the Aegean, the first political threat of consequence for centuries, both shook up the Greek state system and unified it culturally. The emergence of a historical spirit, one by-product of the upheaval, can be seen widely, and in this chapter we shall consider first its manifestations in the arts and literature, especially in Pindar. Thereafter we may look at Herodotus himself as crystallizing the point of view in true history.

THE HISTORICAL SPIRIT IN ARTS AND LETTERS

The arts of the fifth century are not likely to afford obvious illustrations of a historical attitude, both by reason of the very nature of artistic media and also as a consequence of their strong inheritance of mythological and epic subject matter, conventional form, and idealizing drive. So much the more remarkable is the fact that some illustrations do occur.

In Attic pottery the shift from the black-figured style to red-figured technique, about 525 B.C. onward, foreshadowed classical concentration and "lifelike" depiction of characters. In part this new characteristic was due to the technical ability of painters to draw more precise detail inside the areas reserved in red, but to a greater degree the more careful observation of human anatomy and the growingly sensitive exploration of internal human reactions reflected the major change from the archaic to the classic style. The scenes themselves continued largely to be generalized figures of young aristocrats or epic events; occasionally, however, *genre*-like pictures of potters, workers in a foundry, groups of harvesters, and the like demonstrate a conscious interest in the present. Two vases, both in Athens, may be singled out as historically suggestive. One, a mourning scene from a loutrophoros, gives a vivid and concrete sense of grief far beyond the conventionalized pictures of earlier vases (see Plate VI); the Thracian nurse at the head, moreover, is distinctly characterized by tattoo marks on her cheeks.[1] The other, a scene of Heracles assaulting the Egyptian priests of Busiris (see Plate VIIb), likewise underlines the foreign character of the clean-shaven priests and has so strong a narrative sense that we might be misled into thinking the whole event truly historical.

Other vases actually do have connections with historical realities. Some show female characters labeled Sappho; several bear figures called Anacreon—and of these latter some come from the poet's lifetime. The new statues of Harmodius and Aristogeiton were represented on a Würzburg stamnos very soon after their erection; but the most impressive reflection of a real event is the amphora by Myson, c.500–490, which depicts Croesus on his funeral pyre (see Plate IV).[2] Large-scale paintings which were created for the Stoa Poikile (perhaps 462/1 B.C. on) included two mythological scenes, a historical version of the battle of Marathon, and a fourth scene referring to the recent battle of Oinoe.[3]

Nonetheless historical events are not often shown in Attic

[1] Loutrophoros: Athens NM 1170, painter of Kleophrades c.470–60; CVA Greece 2, pl. 80 (Athens 2); Arias-Hirmer, Tausend Jahre griechische Vasenkunst, pl. 129. Heracles pelike: Athens NM 9683, Pan painter; J. D. Beazley, Der Pan-Maler (Berlin, 1931), pl. 7–10.
[2] Sappho: CVA Poland 1, pl. 16.3 (Goluchow), c.500; other examples in Richter, Portraits of the Greeks, p. 71. Anacreon: CVA Denmark 8, pl. 336 (Copenhagen 8), Inv. 13365, by painter of Kleophrades? (Journal of Hellenic Studies, LXXX [1960], p. 203); other examples in Richter, p. 77. Phrynichus: CVA Denmark 8, pl. 351 (Copenhagen 8), Inv. 13817, probably by painter of Kleophon c.425.
  Tyrannicide: Langlotz, Griechische Vasen in Würzburg, p. 103, no. 515; Haspels, Attic Black-figured Lekythoi, p. 167, also about 470; Beazley, Journal of Hellenic Studies, LXVIII (1948), pp. 26–8. Croesus: CVA France 9, pl. 414 (Louvre 6), G 197.
[3] L. H. Jeffery, "The Battle of Oinoe in the Stoa Poikile," Annual of the British School at Athens, LX (1965), pp. 41–57.

pottery. Only through inference can modern scholars assume that the figure of Boreas, which appears occasionally on vases after 480, gained popularity because the north wind seriously damaged the Persian fleet off Euboea; so too the common theme of Amazons fighting Greeks is interpreted as a mythical counterpart to the wars of Persians and Greeks.[4] Insofar as such inferences are correct—and often they rest on very shaky premises—their main utility in the present connection is to suggest how strong was the tendency for vase painters to think in mythical rather than historical terms.

Sculptural styles also changed markedly from the late archaic to the early classic period, while yet remaining bound by earlier conventions as to content. The Athenians commissioned a second group of the tyrannicides, after the Persians had removed the first; and statues of historical personages began slowly to be erected, though only as very generalized figures. The one sculptural work of the fifth century which seems to me to display most consciously a mood akin to the historical is the small, simple relief of Athena leaning on her spear and brooding over a stele; while its meaning is debatable, I would take it that the stele probably listed the names of the dead in a battle (see Plate VIII). If this be correct, the poignant reality of the human costs of empire is evident; it is no great jump to Herodotus' sad observation on the twenty ships which Athens sent to aid the Ionians in 499, "These ships were the beginning of mischief both to the Greeks and to the barbarians."[5]

In literature the alteration in mood and approach from the sixth to the fifth century was marked. Xenophanes the philosopher (*c*.570–475) and Simonides the poet (*c*.556–468) have been singled out in one recent study as standing at the point of change, Xenophanes for his ruthless criticism of fable, Simonides for his intellectual and humane views of man as

---

[4] Boreas: Beazley, *Der Pan-Maler,* p. 11; Instinsky, in *Herodot,* pp. 492–3. Persians and Amazons: see above, p. 52, n. 6.
[5] See above, p. 84, nn. 2–3; Herodotus 5.97.3.

self-moving in his choices; [6] but of all the literary figures who lived about 500 B.C. the poet Pindar (518–438) is most significant for historical purposes. At first sight it may appear unlikely that this composer of epinician odes and other choral works, whose poetry soars into myth and is almost untranslatable in its rich visual imagery, has any connection with history; yet careful consideration of Pindar will uncover remarkable illumination of the mental attitudes which were soon to find historical dress—illumination which is all the more valuable because it is largely unconscious.

As in Herodotus' far-flung story the mental world of Pindar encompasses Babylon and Egypt, Phasis and the Scythians, and the distant Pillars of Heracles. The homeland he visualizes mainly as a congeries of sharply distinct shrines and cities but also as a unified cultural structure; of even the tiny state of Cartheia on the small island of Ceos the poet can proclaim, "I would not exchange this for Babylon." So Hellas will recognize Pindar's genius and the fame of the heroes he celebrates. Pindar's world is a real geographical complex, divided between Hellenic and "barbarian and other-speaking" peoples; it is also significant that for the poet, even more than for Herodotus, the map is bordered by peoples of fable. [7]

Pindar's framework of time is likewise markedly similar to that of Herodotus; no poet down to this point speaks so often of *chronos* itself or other temporal connections. Of the three major temporal divisions, the past appears most often in Pindar as the background of the present; still, it *is* past, an unchanging reality of long dimensions. [8] In keeping with the general tendency of the Greeks to locate perfection in the

[6] Fränkel, *DuP*, pp. 346ff. On choice in Simonides, see Bowra, *Greek Lyric Poetry*, pp. 332ff.; also Lesky, *History of Greek Literature*, pp. 184–90. But in Simonides frr. 63, 66, 100 the gods are still on high.
[7] The boundaries of Pindar's world are given in *Isth.* 2.41–2; *Dithyramb* fr. 82S–96T; *Hyporcheme* fr. 105–6S–121T; *Ol.* 3.44. Cartheia: *Paean* 4. Recognition of Pindar: *Ol.* 1.116, 13.113. Fable: *Isth.* 6.23; *Pyth.* 10.30ff.; *Nem.* 3.21ff., 4.69–70. In discussing Pindar I have drawn on my essay, "Pindar and the Greek Historical Spirit," *Hermes* (forthcoming).
[8] *Pyth.* 2.54, 3.96, 4.55–6; *Ol.* 1.43; fr. 147S–25T.

past—if anywhere—and with Pindar's own penchant for approving aristocratic lineage, the poet at a few points specifically idealizes the past, as in his assertion that men of old did not sell their gifts but that now "money—money is man." Yet here and elsewhere he feels that the nature and quality of past life differed from that of the present, nor was it always perfect.[9] In sum, time brings change.

When Pindar turns to face the future, he finds it a domain far less congenial and certain than the past. Solon and others had observed that men cannot know what will happen hereafter; so too Pindar asserts at several points that we cannot foretell the future. Nevertheless it would be quite incorrect to conclude that his attitude toward the future is one solely of fear. Repeatedly he takes the bold but firm step of promising future fame and glory to mortal men; there is utility in prayer to the gods for the future; and faith in what is to come even leads him to the casual, but significant, assertion that the future will bring out the truth and will save just men.[1]

Pindar thus looks at a world which has a past coming up to his own age, and a future still to arrive, all organically connected but distinguished by temporal terms which reflect fundamental differences. This conscious awareness of time, nonetheless, has an odd, antique flavor; Pindar is in time, but not quite in our kind of time. More specifically, Pindar lacks the modern sense of chronological precision and also views time itself as a living substance.

On the first of these points it is noticeable that, when Pindar does refer to time, he uses only generalized time words; almost always he neglects to give any type of precise dates. Pindar, too, is perfectly capable of moving from the present to the past, of starting near the end of a story, or of jumping about in

[9] *Isth.* 2.1ff.; *Nem.* 8.32; fr. 213S-254T. On the emergence of novelty cf. *Dithyramb* 2; *Ol.* 3.4ff., 13.17, 13.31; *Isth.* 1.26–7; *Nem.* 8.20–1.
[1] Obscurity of future: *Ol.* 2.62, 12.7ff.; *Pyth.* 10.63, 12.30–2; *Nem.* 11.43–4; *Isth.* 3.19. Future fame: *Ol.* 4.10; *Nem.* 4.6. Prayers: *Pyth.* 1.46, 5.117–21, 10.17–8. Truth in future: *Ol.* 1.33–4; fr. 159S-255T; cf. *Ol.* 10.53–4b.

the past without regard for chronological consecutiveness. In the Fourth Pythian, the most notable example, the Argonauts appear first at Cyrene, only thereafter make their journey to Colchis, and finally return to the chronological point at which they first appear. Still, as von Groningen concludes in analyzing the temporal order of three Pindaric odes, "the parts which preserve the natural sequence are always to be found at the end of his narrative." [2] In handling the element of time with this plastic freedom Pindar foreshadows directly the outlook of Herodotus; but when he vivifies time and hails it as "father of all" he clings to the archaic world on a point which Herodotus, if he were to be a historian, could no longer fully accept.[3]

Yet Pindar deals with the deeds of actual men, real figures to be described truthfully against a real background. Like Herodotus he seeks to preserve from decay the happenings of man; his ode is a mirror to give lasting memory to a great deed, for words endure better than events. Achievements of the past, otherwise, go to sleep and are forgotten.[4] Behind both assertions lay an unusual feeling, the deep desire of men in the early fifth century for the preservation of specific events.

A particular victory is always the cause of Pindar's song: "The divine brightness moves, not on some remote battlefield nor even in the pretense of the theatre, but among known scenes of life." [5] Commonly one will find some reference in a Pindaric ode to the place of victory and to the specific contest, as well as the lineage and homeland of the victor. Beside these items, true, there will be a mass of generalization in keeping

[2] *In the Grip of the Past*, p. 44, analyzing the Tenth Nemean, Third Pythian, and Seventh Olympian; cf. Gilbert Norwood, *Pindar* (Berkeley, 1945), p. 86, and John H. Finley, *Pindar and Aeschylus* (Cambridge, Mass., 1955), p. 71.

[3] *Ol.* 2.19; *Nem.* 3.75; fr. 33S-24T; see Hermann Gundert, *Pindar und sein Dichterberuf* (Frankfurt a.M., 1935), p. 130, n. 248.

[4] *Nem.* 4.6, 7.13–6; *Isth.* 7.15ff; Gundert, *Pindar und sein Dichterberuf*, p. 57.

[5] Finley, *Pindar and Aeschylus*, p. 137.

with Pindar's poetic intent as well as with the inherited tendency of Greek thought toward general principles; and always in his odes there are legends. The reasons for which Pindar thus moves from the present into the world of legend and then back again to the present have been fiercely debated in modern scholarship, but the most reasonable suggestion is that the legendary element is fundamentally a comparison to endow a contemporary event with a higher reality. Most certainly the aim is not, as in Hesiod, to explain the present by describing the mythical roots of present forces.[6]

More important, Pindar makes it clear that he alters the myths which he recounts. The motive is at times no doubt a civilized dissatisfaction with a primitive tale, but what Pindar actually says is that the poet must seek the truth; myths "woven with adroit fictions deceive us." Any poet seeking to erect a *monumentum aere perennius* must, we feel, pray with Pindar, "Beginning of great virtue, Truth O Mistress, see to it that never my word breaks on the rock of falsehood." [7] Yet this statement is a landmark in the conscious elevation of truth as an objective principle in early Greek civilization. Neither Pindar's penchant for generalization, in sum, nor his delight in legends carries him completely away from a respect for reality.

Pindar's long life exposed him to the Persian occupation of his native Thebes, to the miraculous liberation of Greece, and to the rising mastery of Athens. While none of this is his primary concern, no poet or philosopher down to his day so clearly manifests the fact that he lives in a historical world. Theognis, for example, dislikes the present but can only grumble and urge his beloved Cyrnus to drink today lest worse befall tomorrow; Solon criticizes and exhorts his fellow Athe-

[6] Snell, *Varia Variorum*, p. 10; Gundert, *Pindar und sein Dichterberuf*, p. 60.
[7] *Ol.* 1.29; fr. 205S-244T. Other passages emphasizing the virtue of truth include *Ol.* 1.28b, 4.17–18, 6.67, 6.89, 10.54–4b; *Pyth.* 3.29–30, 3.103; *Nem.* 1.18, 7.25. In *Pyth.* 1.86 Pindar urges men to pursue the way of truth; cf. Becker, *Das Bild des Weges*, pp. 97–8.

nians in a present almost but not quite timeless. Pindar, however, often turns to the past generations of a victor's family, conjoining past to present in conscious order and seeking to explain present virtue through inheritance of a noble nature from one's ancestors.

Moreover, where Theognis and other earlier poets only occasionally refer to actual historical events, Pindar speaks often of matters about him and at times cites past figures such as Croesus and Archilochus. Even without seeking to wrench historical meanings via allegory, the odes offer abundant illustrations. His Sicilian songs allude to the contemporary battles against Carthaginians and Etruscans, to the foundation of Etna, and in more veiled language to the opposition which Hieron and Theron suffered; for Arcesilaus of Cyrene he is even franker on behalf of the exiled Damophilus. With respect to the Persian invasion he praises the Aeginetan sailors, sighs with relief that this stone of Tantalus has been removed from the head of Greece, and calls violet-crowned Athens the rampart of liberty, whose citizens laid the foundations of liberty at Artemisium.[8] Pindar knows too that societies differ in values and what we may perhaps call customs (*nomima*); one fragment even speaks of "custom, master of the world." This was cited approvingly by Herodotus.

Less personally than Solon, the aristocratic poet of Thebes can also give advice to his contemporaries over all Greece. This advice may be born of his conservative dislike for the changes of the period, but it is couched in humane terms. Pindar favors peace, and has no joy in war, "sweet for those who have not experienced it. But if one knows it, one's heart trembles strangely when it approaches." Here, as the continuing lines show, he is thinking mainly of war born of civil discontent or overweening personal ambitions; and this *stasis*

---

[8] Earlier figures: *Pyth.* 1.94, 2.54ff. Sicily: *Ol.* 2.56–7, 6.97; *Pyth.* 1.30ff., 1.61ff., 3.86ff.; *Nem.* 9.28. Cyrene: *Pyth.* 4 and 5. Persian wars: *Pyth.* 1.76ff.; *Nem.* 1.13?; *Isth.* 5.48ff., 8.9ff.; *Dithyramb* fr. 76S-93T; *Paean* 2. Custom: fr. 169S-187T, 215S-188T; Herodotus 3.38.

turns up elsewhere in his poetry as accursed.[9] The alternative, tranquillity (*Hesychia*), appears as the sovereign blessing both in a fragment of this hyporcheme and especially at the opening of the Eighth Pythian.

Pindar thus treats of men as real figures, who secure specific victories, who are born of a known lineage, who live within a real world. He is proud of his poetic ability, and so too he is proud of mankind's achievements; insofar as he can overcome a realistic Greek suspicion of the unpredictable future he is optimistic. Plato observes that Pindar pictured men as measuring the regions above the earth and the stars; in the enthusiastic outburst of the poet that "there are many marvels in the world" one may detect that mental outlook which could attach importance to the events recorded in formal history.[1]

All this we may rightly account a necessary part of the intellectual environment in which written history emerged, even though Pindar himself was no historian; purely as a poet he was almost always chary of the piquant detail which our modern minds have long been trained to expect in accounts of reality. One major question remains: how can any man who places the basic responsibility for human actions in the hands of the gods be associated with a truly historical spirit?

For beside and above Pindar's celebration of the virtue (*arete*) of terrestrial men, inherited from their aristocratic forebears and exhibited in glorious victory, stands the divine will, which is the ultimate mover. In ode after ode this is one of the major themes. Zeus is master of all, who gives now successes, now reverses; only with the aid of the gods can man rise; and man's wisdom (*sophia*) cannot hope to sound the will of the gods—"Alas, how much does the thought of ephemeral man err in its ignorance!" Moreover, it is dangerous for a

[9] War: *Hyporcheme* fr. 268S-120T. Stasis: *Pyth.* 5.66–7; *Paean* 9; fr. 210S-250T. Praise of tranquillity: *Ol.* 4.16; *Hyporcheme* fr. 109–10S-120T; *Nem.* 1.70. *Ol.* 13.7 celebrates Eirene; *Ol.* 9.16 and 13.6, Eunomia.
[1] Plato, *Theaetetus* 173E; *Ol.* 1.28.

man to struggle with the more powerful beings above, for divine jealousy is easily aroused.[2]

As we have observed before, this is a conventional picture; and, though a true representation of early Greek views of the divine, it is singularly liable to distortion when approached in a modern, rationalistic mood. For Pindar it would be easy to create a convincing picture of divine omnipotence and human subjection—only to find that he, no less than Homer or Sophocles, does not cravenly fear the gods. Pindar can call them good, and suggests in the Sixth Nemean that men and gods, though different in race, are of the same Mother Earth. Mankind, he continues, is naught, but we have some relation with the gods in mind or nature. That obscurely unpredictable force, *Tyche*, can determine success or failure, with or apart from divine will.[3]

Most important of all, men *do* produce the earthly results of history. If only they have liberty, they can counter the effects of perfidious time.[4] In the Fifth Isthmian, Zeus is said to have sent the murderous rain of Salamis—but the sailors of Aegina saved the Greeks. However wildly inconsistent the assertion may appear, it is a typically Greek juxtaposition. Herodotus, as well as Pindar, firmly believed in divine mastery, which caused the fall of Xerxes through *hybris;* and yet praised the Athenians as the principal earthly cause of the Greek success.

Of all the early fifth-century authors Pindar comes closest to the outlook which spurred Herodotus and gave the Father of History his audience. But Pindar does not stand alone. The same views of space and time, of man's achievements, and of the overarching divine mastery of the earthly scene can be

---

[2] Divine control: *Isth.* 5.52–53; *Nem.* 10.29; *Paean* 13; fr. 182S-209T, 209S-248T. Examples of divine aid: *Ol.* 7.51–2, 9.28, 9.103–4, 10.20–1; *Pyth.* 8.75–7; 1.41; fr. 140S-145T, 141S-146T. Jealousy: *Ol.* 5.23–4b; *Pyth.* 10.20–1; *Nem.* 10.72, 11.45–8.
[3] *Isth.* 4.31; *Nem.* 10.26; fr. 38S-167T. Cf. Degani, AIΩN, p. 58; Guthrie, *Greek Philosophy*, I, pp. 142–3; II, pp. 161–3, 414–17.
[4] *Isth.* 8.15.

found in duller form in the odes of Simonides' nephew Bacchylides;[5] they also appear in Attic tragedy, as in the plays of Pindar's contemporary Aeschylus. To repeat for Aeschylus the analysis which has been advanced for Pindar would be unnecessary; and since I have cited the evidence of the tragedian at appropriate points in previous chapters a brief recapitulation of his position may suffice here.

For Aeschylus the *polis* furnishes the background of political and social virtues. Especially in the *Suppliants* this is true, but elsewhere as well the public forms an audience of considerable weight.[6] Men are responsible for their actions under the rule of the gods; Aeschylus can praise man's achievements while also emphasizing the dangers of *hybris*. The tragedian transports his audience far afield and perhaps visualizes the dimension of space more clearly than did Pindar; but in the area of time his evidence is far less significant. The present usually outweighs all else; the past is only occasionally noted; and the future rises as a concern principally in the *Eumenides*. Words such as *chronos* appear far more rarely in Aeschylus than in Pindar, save in the *Agamemnon* and *Eumenides*, though Aeschylus too is aware that change comes in time.[7]

The great characters of his tragedies move across the stage as members of an idealized world which lacks direct connection with the life of the fifth century; one is reminded of the

[5] Bacchylides uses inversion in *Ep.* 11, notes the distinction of past and present in fr. 5, and views time as an active agent (*Ep.* 13.205–6, ὅτε πανδαμάτωρ/χρόνος, cf. Simonides fr. 5); but he lacks the wealth of temporal terms evident in Pindar. His one historical reference is *Ep.* 3.27, to Croesus; nor does Bacchylides show the intense political sense of Pindar. Rather he spends more time on the actual event and the athletic prowess of the victor, as in *Ep.* 10. On his concept of *Aletheia*, cf. references in Gundert, *Pindar und sein Dichterberuf*, p. 130 n. 248.
[6] E.g., *Persians* 591ff. (but cf. 213); *Agamemnon* 456ff., 1355ff.
[7] Thus change is admitted in the final chorus of the *Seven Against Thebes* (1076–7): "What a State approves as just changes with changing times." See *Eumenides* 853 (286 may be spurious); *Choephori* 965, which has *chronos* as the subject (as also *Agamemnon* 982). Cf. generally Accame, *Rivista di filologia*, n.s. XXXIX (1961), pp. 388–90. For space in Aeschylus, see Chapter II.

observation about the epic characters on vases: "under their sculptured forms beat the hearts not of men, but of Man."[8] Tragedy and history are parallel, independent developments out of the tradition of the epic and lyric poets; for the occasional effort to make Clio the daughter of Melpomene has no fundamental justification.

Rather, the historical spirit found more significant sustenance in that interest in specific fact which led to works in geography, ethnography, and medicine; the strongest theoretical statements of the attitudes which directed Herodotus' inquiries are the Hippocratic treatises *On Airs Waters Places* and *On Ancient Medicine*. Their evidence has already been considered and need not be repeated, but it must always be kept in mind.

HERODOTUS, FATHER OF HISTORY

The Greek audiences of the fifth century were subject to many influences of diverse character. These came down out of the archaic period but assumed specialized, independent forms of existence at this point. Especially of the Athenians, in Aristotle's words, "their achievements, in the period of the Persian wars and afterwards, had elated their pride; and anxious only to explore fresh fields they took all studies indiscriminately for their province."[9]

To meet one need of this world there appeared at Athens somewhere in the 440's Herodotus of Halicarnassus. Born about 485 B.C., he had lived for a time at Samos, where presumably he acquired his knowledge of Ionian speculation; he had traveled to Egypt, Babylon, and the Black Sea. Although the history which he now wrote, and at least in part recited, culminated in the Persian invasions of 490–79, its greater part was devoted to the rise of the Persians and a more

[8] Selincourt, *World of Herodotus*, p. 318.
[9] Aristotle, *Politics* 8.6.11 (1341a.28–32) (tr. Barker).

or less lengthy description of the peoples whom the Persians conquered, in chronological sequence. The *History* of Herodotus is in some ways a *Persica;* certainly its main thread is not that of Greek developments, which are interwoven at relevant points in his gradually unfolding tale.[1]

Rarely has there been so marvelous a coincidence of a greatly gifted man and the felicitous occasion. This is not to say that Herodotus exhibited keen analytical powers of a high order, as did Thucydides; in lieu thereof he possessed a phenomenal memory, lively curiosity harnessed by skepticism, warm sympathy coupled with unusual objectivity. These qualities, as applied to his subject within an inherited framework of epic tradition and archaic literary style, made his history a unique creation, never repeated in antiquity. His audience, too, was unusual in the degree to which it was ready to listen to a historical composition; we are told that he stirred the young Thucydides and received a public present of ten talents.[2] Even more significant is the fact that his work was preserved, the earliest extensive piece of Greek prose to survive.

Before we consider his historical qualities, a few general observations are required to set Herodotus in the proper framework. The common assertion that he was led to write history rather than geography—and to choose the subject he did—by residence in Athens puts the matter in too narrow

[1] Regenbogen, in *Herodot,* p. 75 (after Creuzer); de Sanctis, *Studi di storia,* pp. 21–45. On the unity of his work, cf. H. Erbse, "Tradition und Form im Werke Herodots," *Gymnasium,* LXVIII (1961), pp. 239–57. In general, see Selincourt, *World of Herodotus; Herodot,* ed. W. Marg, which collects some valuable recent essays; the reports of Paul MacKendrick, *Classical Weekly,* XLVII (1954), pp. 145–52; *Classical World,* LVI (1963), pp. 269–75. The long study by F. Jacoby, in PW *s.v.* Herodotos (Supplementband II, 1913), is better in its detail than in its general judgment. Some other recent work is cited below; but I cannot hope to be inclusive or to take into account all the varied views which have been advanced.

[2] Marcellinus, *vita Thucydidis* 54; Plutarch, *de Herodoti malignitate* 26; cf. Strasburger, in *Herodot,* p. 575, for other evidence and modern discussions.

terms; the course of Greek history itself is often distorted by an overemphasis on Athens. The concentration and endurance which Herodotus needed to complete so mammoth a task may well have been facilitated by the encouragement he received from interested Athenians. This interest in the past, in turn, owed much to that sense of personal responsibility interwoven in Attic thought since Solon and also to that pride in the Persian defeat and subsequent Athenian empire which fired Pericles' fellow citizens. But these are not the ultimate roots of Herodotus' historical attitude. A gentle commentator on Herodotus has perhaps put the relationship best in observing that "his preference for Athens was a necessary consequence of his general outlook upon life and the world, of his own liberal and inquiring mind." [3]

We simply cannot limit the problems involved in the actual emergence of history to the personal characteristics of Herodotus himself or to the interest which the Athenians may have shown in his tale of the Persian defeat. Pherecydes had already written at Athens on myths, genealogies, and so forth; this work, though not composed in a really historical manner, nonetheless manifested a sober interest in the past. Hellanicus of Mitylene was drawn by the pull of the Aegean capital soon after Herodotus and there poured out a mass of monographs on chronology, the early history of Attica, mythography, Egypt, Persia, and other subjects.[4] Nor did Athens furnish the only audience, for two other historians flourished elsewhere

[3] Selincourt, *World of Herodotus*, p. 44, cf. pp. 31, 42–3; see also H. Strasburger, "Herodot und das perikleische Athen," in *Herodot*, pp. 574–608, and H. Kleinknecht, "Herodot und Athen," ibid., pp. 541–73. The usual picture: Peter, *Wahrheit und Kunst*, pp. 79–81, 93–7; more generally on the significance of Athens, Jaeger, *Paideia*, I, pp. 188–9.

[4] Pherecydes: R. Laqueur, in PW *s.v.* Pherekydes; Jacoby, *Abhandlungen*, pp. 100–43, dates him before 476/5 B.C. Hellanicus: Pearson, *Early Ionian Historians*, pp. 152ff., and *Local Historians of Attica*, pp. 1ff.; Jacoby, *FGrH*, no. 4, and Dritter Teil.B (Supplement I) (Leiden, 1954), pp. 1–21. His influence is traced by Jacoby, *Atthis: The Local Chronicles of Ancient Athens* (Oxford, 1949); a new argument on his date is advanced by F. P. Rizzo, "Sulla cronologia della vita di Ellanico," *Athenaeum*, n.s. XLIII (1963), pp. 369–84.

very shortly after Herodotus. At Lampsacus, Charon wrote some sort of history; in Syracuse, Antiochus established a chronological framework for Sicilian history, on which Thucydides later drew. Antiochus, moreover, was clear enough on the principles of historical criticism to state at the outset of his work on Italy that he selected "from old tales the most worthy of belief and clearest information." [5]

The tone of Herodotus' history clearly shows that he thought much of Greece would be interested in the fruit of his researches. True, the Athenians were themselves indefatigable in preserving the memory of those who fought the Persians, by erecting the mound at Marathon as well as monuments at Marathon and Salamis and epigrams in the Agora; Aeschylus wished to be remembered as a "Marathon-fighter." [6] They were, however, not alone in this pride. The Corinthians set up a monument at Salamis; the Spartans commissioned an epigram by Simonides for Thermopylae; further memorials were due to the Megarians and others; and all the allied Greeks were listed on the tripod at Delphi, the base of which still survives. [7] In any case Herodotus did not need to come to Athens to be aware of the Persian Empire, under whose rule he was born at Halicarnassus. All that we can be sure of is that, however he chose his subject, it did not displease his Athenian—and Greek—audience.

[5] Charon: Jacoby, *Abhandlungen*, pp. 178–206; A. Hepparle, "Charon von Lampsakos," *Festschrift Regenbogen* (Heidelberg, 1956), pp. 67–76. Antiochus: Schwartz in PW *s.v.* Antiochos (60); *FGrH*, no. 555; G. de Sanctis, *Ricerche sulla storiografia siceliota* (Palermo, 1958), pp. 9–16.
[6] Athenaeus 14.627c = Peek no. 43; Tod, *GHI*, I, nos. 13, 14, 18, 21; B. D. Meritt, "Epigrams from the Battle of Marathon," *The Aegean and the Near East* (Locust Valley, N.Y., 1956), pp. 268–80; Dorothy Burr Thompson, "The Persian Spoils in Athens," ibid., pp. 281–91; Eugene Vanderpool, "A Monument to the Battle of Marathon," *Hesperia*, XXXV (1966), pp. 93–106, which he dates c.475–50. On the Eion epigrams see Meritt, loc. cit.; Aeschines 3.183–5; Plutarch, *Cimon* 7.
[7] Tod, *GHI*, I, nos. 19, 20, 16 (cf. A. L. Boegehold, "The Salamis Epigram," *Greek, Roman, and Byzantine Studies*, VI [1965], pp. 179–86, against Rhys Carpenter, *American Journal of Archaeology*, LXVII [1963], p. 209).

In the present connection I cannot consider Herodotus at the length he deserves. The observation of Gomme that "he more than most writers is one to read, not to talk about," has its point; but still Herodotus is the subject of a continuing host of specialized essays and large-scale works, the general tendency of which has been to redeem his reputation from its depreciation in the nineteenth century.[8] Yet a few comments must be made, not to explain Herodotus himself but rather to show how he drew together the threads we have thus far followed. Since he has been far too often misunderstood in these matters, I shall deliberately accentuate the evidence for the presence of a real historical spirit in his work.

As far as the treatment of space is concerned, this is so prominent in Herodotus' history as to occasion an argument that his original intent was purely geographic and ethnographic, in the tradition of Hecataeus' *Periegesis*.[9] Herodotus traveled widely and everywhere sought detailed information, though like all travelers he was occasionally at the mercy of fanciful guides. His distances and directions are not always correct, but he is dealing with a real, variegated world. In the Ionian tradition he seeks natural causes for major geological developments, and in an interesting passage on the formation of the Delta he is capable of projecting the deposits of the Nile both back and also forward in the future for an estimated ten or twenty thousand years. Although Herodotus' effort is to ascertain geographical fact, the innate Greek tendency to think symmetrically does reflect itself in his construction of the paths of Danube and Nile as parallel, north and south, in the unknown regions of Europe and Africa.

Some later writers criticized him as partial to the barbarians, a remarkable misconstruction; for in the speeches of king

[8] Gomme, *Greek Attitude to Poetry and History*, p. 94.
[9] See generally J. L. Myres, *Herodotus* (Oxford, 1953), pp. 32–59. R. M. Macan, *Herodotus: The Seventh, Eighth, and Ninth Books* (London, 1908), I, pp. xlv–lxi, argued that Books 7–9 were written first (as also Gomme, *Greek Attitude to Poetry and History*, p. 78).

Demaratus and elsewhere he displays deep Hellenic loyalty. No less than Aeschylus, who fought against the foe, Herodotus can treat the Persians with objectivity, and amply illuminates the treachery and divided counsels of the Greeks; so too he can respect the antiquity of Egyptian civilization and assert that the Greeks had borrowed much thence.[1] Yet the Persians are slaves of an arbitrary despot, to be driven into battle by a lash, while the Greeks are "free men owning no master but the Law."

Few later writers, save perhaps Posidonius, were to show as wide an interest in foreign peoples and lands while still encompassing their material within a historical framework. *Chronos* is the thirteenth word in his introduction; then come, in temporal succession, the mutual raids of easterners and Greeks for women; and thereafter the story unfolds in fundamentally chronological fashion. The past and present are different, a point which he emphasizes in the theory, stated at the end of his preface, that human happiness never remains long in the same place; therefore Herodotus will write of big and little cities alike, the great states now having once been minor.[2] Always Herodotus is interested in origins of customs and institutions, and seeks to date them. Homer and Hesiod do not float in a temporal void but "lived but four hundred years before my time, as I believe. As for the poets, who are thought by some to be earlier than these, they are, in my judgment, decidedly later writers." From Herodotus more than any other source, except perhaps the *Chronicon* of Euse-

---

[1] Barbarian partiality: Plutarch, *de Herodoti malignitate* 11–14 (856D-857F); but cf. Herodotus 1.60.3, 4.95.2, 7.11.3, 7.104, 7.135. See the judicious remarks of J. Vogt, "Herodot in Ägypten," in *Herodot*, pp. 412–33; Selincourt, *World of Herodotus*, pp. 78–80.

[2] Herodotus 1.5.3–4. To list all examples of change in time would require an essay; see 1.57.2–3 for the Athenians themselves, or for the Scythians 4.5.1 and 4.8.1, or for the wastage of time 7.176.5. In 5.9.3 he observes, γένοιτο δ'ἂν πᾶν ἐν τῷ μακρῷ χρόνῳ. See generally H. Strasburger, "Herodots Zeitrechnung," in *Herodot*, pp. 677–725; Fordyce Mitchel, "Herodotus' Use of Genealogical Chronology," *Phoenix*, X (1956), pp. 48–69.

bius, stems our chronological picture of early Greece; and one would deeply like to know how he could take two entirely different chains of events, such as those remembered at Proconnesus and Metapontum, to establish synchronisms.[3] In what is yet to come Herodotus is not greatly interested, but at several points we can see his view that the future comes out of the present as well as a sense of the insecurity of man's life which reminds one of Pindar.[4]

His time, like that of Pindar, is not quite ours. Time is measured often in general words, at times by generations, only occasionally by a specific number of years; the one formal date is that of the Persian burning of Athens, in the archonship of Calliades. Herodotus, too, has a fondness for telling the end of a story first and then going back in archaic inversion; his whole work, while basically a forward progress in time as the Persians conquered first one, then another people, can spiral on its line so as to give the earlier history of, say, Egypt and related events of previous eras in Greek history. If time means change, this does not entail a belief that the change has always been continuous; especially in discussing customs Herodotus often takes them as timeless. It is small wonder that several otherwise careful scholars have actually denied Herodotus any sense of time, in the sense of firm, specific chronology; but these students are seeking what Herodotus could not have given in view of the knowledge of his day.[5] On the fundamental, significant point one must be clear:

[3] Herodotus 2.53.2; 4.15.1. Note the correlations in 5.44.1, 5.97.1, 5.108.1, 9.7.1.

[4] So in the famous debate on the Persian form of government (3.80ff.) results are predicted for each form of government; Miltiades predicts the results from fighting at Marathon (6.109.3–6); envoys tell Gelon the Persians will attack him next (7.157.3). Cf. 3.62.4, 3.65.3 (fated from omens), 6.67.3, 6.85.2. Foreshadowing also appears in 5.97.3, 5.92.η5, etc. In 6.98.1, 9.64.1, and elsewhere the phrase "of those events which we know" (τῶν ἡμεῖς ἴδμεν) suggests Herodotus' awareness that the future might bring forth new information or events. Insecurity: 1.32, 1.86, 3.40ff., 6.86.α3.

[5] Herodotus 8.51.1. Observe the difficulty in telling time in 4.98; in setting an hour, Herodotus can say only, "the time when the market-

Herodotus interpreted the situation of the world in his time as the result of change in the past, and felt that this change could be described; of all the thinkers we know he is the first to have carried out his belief in written history.

Two further aspects of time in Herodotus should be noted. One rises from the modern insistence that the Greeks viewed time as cyclical; and here I may simply observe that, while Herodotus once talks of the affairs of individual men as a "circle," the tale he tells is not in any respect constructed on a cyclical scheme. Even for Thucydides, who had strong feelings about the sameness of human nature as a proof of the utility of his history, Gomme is certainly right, "To say that he believed that similar events would recur is not to say that he believed that events go round in cycles." [6] The second point with respect to Herodotus is the fact that in his story, unlike the odes of Pindar, time is not an independent force. It is simply a dimension of his tale, and the motive forces lie elsewhere.

His history is one of men organized in states—Greek *poleis,* native kingdoms, and the realm of the Persian Great King—all situated within a real landscape. Of the twenty most frequent common nouns in his work, four refer to human beings, six to states and their armaments, four to geographical features, two to time, and only one to matters divine; his introduction,

---

place is wont to fill" (7.223.1). Note also the lack of awareness of the speed of a development in 7.206.2, 9.77. In Tod, *GHI,* I, no. 25, on the other hand, a specific month is given for the decree and a time limit of eighteen months is placed on claims—from Halicarnassus, Herodotus' birthplace, c. 460–55. Inversion: Strasburger, in *Herodot,* pp. 582–83; Gomme, *Greek Attitude to Poetry and History,* p. 76; van Groningen, *In the Grip of the Past,* pp. 38–42; on his use of γάρ, see van Groningen, *La Composition archaïque,* pp. 19–20.
[6] Gomme, *Greek Attitude to Poetry and History,* p. 156; see also Vidal-Naquet, *Revue de l'histoire des religions,* CLVII (1960), pp. 69–70; van Leyden, *Durham University Journal,* XI (1950), pp. 97–104; and Gomme's *Commentary* on Thucydides 3.82.
On time as an independent force in Herodotus, *chronos* seems to be the subject alone only in 1.61.4; in 1.160.5 etc. it is the subject with *oligos* and so on. Both uses are temporal, not causative. Circle: 1.207.

significantly enough, speaks solely of men and does not invoke supernatural help either in composing his story or in finding the truth.[7]

To discuss fully Herodotus' view of man would involve a recounting of his history, which concerns men and especially great men in their human and political roles. As he states in his preface, his aim is to explain the "causes" for their confrontation as East and West; the pattern of causation which follows is human. The twenty ships sent by the Athenians to help the Ionian rebels were "the beginning of mischief"; pride, ambition, passion, and fallibility—all play their part along with those uncertain causes which any historian must meet in seeking to account for the medley of history. On the major factors at work alike in political and military affairs Herodotus has in general a penetrating insight even though he is willing, for the details, to accept or to recount unbelievable stories.[8]

Here again his view of man is not quite ours. His figures tend to be generalized, much as those in archaic and classical sculpture. In their delineation as well as in his general style the Homeric influence is quite visible, not yet checked by the sophistic analysis of human nature (*physis*) and a clear sense of human individuality. Economic factors rarely play a role. Above all, the gods drive Xerxes to his fall or Polycrates to his crucifixion; Herodotus, no less than archaic poets and philosophers, sees the hand of the gods in human actions though he is too empirical a historian to view the whole process as directly

---

[7] J. E. Powell, A Lexicon to Herodotus (2d ed.; Hildesheim, 1966): human beings, ἀνήρ 771 times, παῖς 410, γυνή 373, ἄνθρωπος 307; states and armaments, βασιλεύς 624, πόλις 469, νῆυς 404, στρατός 221, στρατιή 218, ἵππος 205; geographical features, χώρη 339, ποταμός 322, γῆ 265, θάλασσα 229; time, χρόνος 295, ἡμέρη 280; divine, θεός 272, in fourteenth place. The other three most frequent common nouns are λόγος 447, οὔνομα 277, πρῆγμα 210.

[8] A. Ferrill, "Herodotus and the Strategy and Tactics of the Invasion of Xerxes," American Historical Review, LXXII (1966), pp. 102–15; Gomme, Greek Attitude to Poetry and History, pp. 105–12; Lionel Pearson, "Credulity and Scepticism in Herodotus," Transactions of the American Philological Association, LXXII (1941), pp. 333–55.

ethical in motivation.[9] This religious belief is perhaps the main factor which has led recent students to elevate Thucydides over Herodotus; but in the pattern of Greek civilization as it had developed from Homer through Pindar could we reasonably expect otherwise?

Nor, against this background, need we conclude—as is sometimes argued—that Herodotus draws his views of man from tragedy, as though this were the source of all thought about mankind in the fifth century; or that history is simply epic in another form, the epic cycle now being closed.[1] Naturally Herodotus shares many ideas with the contemporary tragedians; naturally, too, his childhood training left a strong epic imprint on Herodotus' thought, as it did for Thucydides and many later historians. But Herodotus is writing about real men always, and the immediate causes of his tale are in human terms.

Herodotus, to reiterate an earlier comment, was not a giant if we measure his work in its sheer powers of reason; but this is an inappropriate measure for historians of any age. Far more important are instinctive sympathy, imagination, and understanding; and these qualities Herodotus possessed in abundance. On the other side we must not underestimate the intellectual qualities of his work. His scheme is as wide-sweeping as the cosmological pictures of the early philosophers; and probably, had we their works, we should find that

[9] Meyer, in *Herodot*, pp. 12–20; M. P. Nilsson, *Geschichte der griechischen Religion*, I (2d ed.; Munich, 1955), pp. 735, 759–67; G. C. J. Daniels, *Religieus-historische Studie over Herodotus* (Antwerp-Nijmegen, 1946); W. Pötscher, "Götter und Gottheit bei Herodot," *Wiener Studien*, LXXI (1958), pp. 5–29; Strasburger, *Die Wesensbestimmung der Geschichte*, pp. 70–1.

[1] Tragedy: Jacoby in PW *s.v.* Herodotos, col. 488; Hans Fohl, *Tragische Kunst bei Herodot* (Diss. Rostock, 1913); F. W. Walbank, "History and Tragedy," *Historia*, IX (1960), pp. 216–34; K. H. Waters, "The Purpose of Dramatisation in Herodotus," *Historia*, XV (1966), pp. 157–71. Epic: Pearson, *Early Ionian Historians*, p. 15; Strasburger, *Die Wesensbestimmung der Geschichte*, pp. 62–9; Jacoby in PW *s.v.* Herodotos, cols. 491–2; Wolf Aly, *Volksmärchen, Sage und Novelle bei Herodot und seinen Zeitgenossen* (Göttingen, 1921), pp. 266–77.

they too interwove digressions within a basically systematic arrangement. Repeatedly Herodotus erects signposts to indicate that this or that matter will be referred to later, or has already been taken up.[2] His tale is, moreover, not simply a recital of events; he analyzes, contrasts pretext and reality, and on occasion constructs "models" or hypotheses to aid in reaching the truth, as in treating the causes of the Nile flood.[3]

Here we reach one of the fundamental bases for judging any historian; but any effort to assess Herodotus' attitude toward the truth simply in the light of modern historical theory will go badly astray. If Herodotus could only have introduced his work with a few brief but pithy paragraphs, like those in which Thucydides discussed the difficulty of establishing the truth and proclaimed his own zeal in ferreting it out, we should be likely to think much better of the Father of History; but alas! he actually commences with a faradiddle of women-stealing and thereafter never passes over an amazing or peculiar tale which strikes his fancy, unlikely though it may be. In these respects, to speak more seriously, he was the heir of that archaic outlook which we have already investigated. Even had he desired to do so, he could not actually have spoken with Thucydides' clarity; the methods of research at his disposal also hampered his *conscious* concentration on the truth.

In Herodotean usage therefore the concept of absolute truth has only a limited place. As I observed in Chapter V above, the archaic era was tinged with a deep pessimism about human fallibility, and even philosophers were inclined to seek especially coherence in their theories above all else. Very

[2] In Book 1 alone cf. 5.3, 75.1, 95.1, 106.2, 130.3, 140.3. See W. A. A. van Otterlo, "Untersuchungen über Begriff, Anwendung und Entstehung der griechischen Ringkomposition," *Mededeelingen der Nederlandsche Akademie van Wetenschappen,* Afdeeling letterkunde, n.s. 7/3 (Amsterdam, 1944).

[3] Herodotus 2.20–2, 4.167.3, 7.138.1, etc. Cf. H. Kleinknecht, in *Herodot,* pp. 546–9.

rarely, as a result, does Herodotus proclaim anything unmistakably true; more often, it is *atrekes,* a term which means "exact" or "precise" in the first instance, or it may be *alethes,* a companion adjective to *logos,* to indicate true transmission.[4] Herodotus' methods of research probably owed much to those of Hecataeus, who traveled widely and sought information from local informants; for these were his own principal sources, though he read inscriptions and such written materials as were available. How Herodotus kept this material, garnered over years, in his head we do not know; but it is most unlikely that he had at his disposal a pack of formal notes. As a result he can make even simple mistakes on the factual level. For this any historian with a sense of humility must forgive him; what matters more is that Herodotus is far less concerned with absolute precision than is demanded by modern historical method.

All this granted, the truth is nonetheless a deeply important aspect in Herodotus, and his critical spirit differs from that of Thucydides not in quality but in its instinctive, as against conscious, presence. The demand for truth, indeed, affects Herodotus' approach in several significant respects. He was always searching, as he states himself, to collect information so that the great deeds of the Greeks and barbarians should not perish. The main aim being an assembly of tales (*logoi*), Herodotus might well have been a mere antiquarian or encyclopaedist; he specifically observes, "My duty is to report all that is said, but I am not obliged to believe it all alike—a remark which may be understood to apply to my whole History." [5] But his own innate genius, combined with the emerging historical interests of his age, leads him to ask and to answer great questions, to organize and assay information

[4] See Powell, *Lexicon, svv.* especially 7.139.1, 8.8.2–3; Schadewaldt, in *Herodot,* p. 115.
[5] Herodotus 7.152; cf. 2.123.1, "For my own part, I propose to myself throughout my whole work faithfully to record the traditions of the several nations." Also significant is 6.55.

143

drawn from many types of sources, to tell the legends (as of early Scythia) and then to settle on a more prosaic and realistic account.[6] In his description of Egypt Herodotus thus marks sharply the distinction between evidence based on his own inspection, judgment, and inquiries on the one hand and inherited tradition on the other. Herodotus, in brief, is not simply a recording device. On occasion he can go so far as to tell opposing stories and suspend judgment as to which is true; and if it be the true mark of a historian that he criticizes his predecessors we must remember that Herodotus censures Hecataeus more often than Thucydides in turn criticizes Herodotus.

The search for truth also directs his choice of subject matter away from the conventional material surveyed by such predecessors as Hecataeus, Acusilaus, and Pherecydes. Apart from the introduction, magniloquent to gain attention, he shuns the world of Greek myth and epic; rather, as he states, "I shall proceed at once to point out the person who first within my own knowledge commenced aggressions on the Greeks." His history, in consequence, rarely goes back in any detail much before the middle of the sixth century, evidently the limit in his judgment of his informants' knowledge, though in matters of lineage he may plunge further.[7] Of Minos' thalassocracy, to give one fascinating example, he is clearly dubious and asserts that Polycrates "was the first of mere human birth who conceived the design of gaining the empire of the sea"; Thucydides, on the other hand, accepts the myth of Minos' power

[6] Herodotus 4.5–12, 1.95, 2.14. Note the complicated strands of the Croesus tale: O. Regenbogen, "Die Geschichte von Solon und Krösus," in *Herodot*, pp. 375–403; Hellmann, *Neue Philologische Untersuchungen*, IX; G. de Sanctis, "Il 'Logos' di Creso e il proemio della storia erodotea," *Studi di storia*, pp. 48–71. Egypt: Herodotus 2.99.1. A few other examples of his critical spirit may be given: 1.57, 1.75, 2.103–05, 3.115, 5.85–7, 8.119. On his use of inscriptions see H. Volkmann, "Die Inschriften im Geschichtswerk des Herodots," *Convivium* (Stuttgart, 1954), pp. 41–65.

[7] Herodotus 8.131.2, 8.44.2, 8.73; cf. 1.145, 5.82ff.

and rationalizes it as a "natural desire to protect his growing revenues." [8] This skepticism of Herodotus was perhaps naïve, and certainly his reputation for veracity did not stand high in antiquity; but in the end his work is based on the unwritten assumption that history, if it is to be valuable, must fundamentally be true.

Parallel to his efforts at determining the truth is his basic objectivity. Unlike many historians and poets of later times he does not idealize the past; he can describe alien customs dispassionately. Still, Herodotus on occasion promenades his own firm conclusions, as in a famous passage in Book Seven:

> Here I feel constrained to deliver an opinion, which most men, I know, will dislike, but which, as it seems to me to be true, I am determined not to withhold. Had the Athenians, from fear of the approaching danger, quitted their country, or had they without quitting it submitted to the power of Xerxes, there would certainly have been no attempt to resist the Persians by sea . . . If then a man should now say that the Athenians were the saviours of Greece, he would not exceed the truth . . . next to the gods, they repulsed the invader.[9]

Written at a time when the Athenian empire was much hated in the Aegean, this judgment, and the reasoning which goes to support it, is superb testimony to his impartiality; but it can be matched elsewhere in his treatment of the Persians or of Spartan valor. Like any historian Herodotus is occasionally misled by his sources, as in his denigration of Themistocles; and again, like all historical students, he has innate, unconscious prejudices—pro-Hellene in essence, mocking to the Ionians, and so on. But any effort to make him an apologist for

[8] Herodotus 3.122; Thucydides 1.4. Further criticisms of myth may be found, e.g., in 4.8ff., 6.53. Ancient criticism: A. Momigliano, "The Place of Herodotus in the History of Historiography," *Studies in Historiography*, pp. 127–42 (cf. pp. 211–20).
[9] Herodotus 7.139. Cf. 8.73.3, "If I may speak freely," then he must state that other Peloponnesian states, being neutral, really Medized.

Athens must shatter on dispassionate reading of his history; it cannot even be proved that he admired Pericles.[1]

Finally, his history is an extraordinarily rich tapestry of human life, lit by the glow of a warm heart, which overpasses the sense of sorrow, human fallibility, and inevitable passing-away which he also knew. Pessimism about mortal existence is the normal companion of the true historian. And the tale is clothed in an outwardly running narrative, a marvelous style which hides cunning artifice, as in the speeches; [2] the skills of formal Greek rhetoric were only to be made conscious by the sophists.

If Herodotus is an archaic man, as he is sometimes labeled, then we must conclude that the necessary qualities for a historical outlook had been fashioned in the archaic period. Herodotus assembled them, and his audience comprehended the result. Next came Thucydides, who set ancient historiography in its pattern of annalistic treatment and preference for the limitation of content to contemporary political and military events. History became the poorer for these restrictions, but then such a genius as Herodotus has rarely served Clio.[3]

[1] Gomme, *Greek Attitude to Poetry and History*, pp. 111–15; Strasburger, in *Herodot*, pp. 574ff.; F. D. Harvey, "The Political Sympathies of Herodotus," *Historia*, XV (1966), pp. 254–5, disagrees.

[2] Aristotle, *Rhetoric* 3.9 (1409a.27); van Groningen, *La Composition archaïque*, pp. 236–7; J. D. Denniston, in *Herodot*, p. 743; L. Solmsen, ibid. pp. 629ff.; Regenbogen, ibid. pp. 77–9.

Pessimism: Herodotus 1.32, 7.46; still it is better to try (7.50), and man works best when he is free (5.78).

[3] In this judgment I do not deny great ability to Thucydides himself; but it remains true that Herodotus had a deeper sense of the web of history. I thus disagree completely with Chatelet, *La Naissance de l'histoire*, p. 222, that his history "au vrai, n'excède guère la simple transcription du passé comme tel." See also the comparisons of Herodotus and Thucydides by H. Strasburger, "Die Entdeckung der politischen Geschichte durch Thukydides," *Saeculum*, V (1954), pp. 395–428, and *Die Wesensbestimmung der Geschichte*.

CHAPTER 7

THE ONWARD MARCH

OF HISTORY

ЛЛЛЛЛЛЛЛЛЛЛЛЛЛЛЛЛЛЛЛЛЛЛЛЛ

DURING THE LATER DECADES of the fifth century men's interest in their own nature and deeds was considerably broadened. The sophists explored the distinction between *nomos*
and *physis;* Alcibiades and Socrates, each in his own manner,
asserted their individuality; Ion of Chios and Stesimbrotus of
Thasos found it useful to set down tales of their contemporaries.

A variety of physical testimonials also suggests a growth in
concern for previous events. The first inscription which gives
specific detail of a man's career is the tombstone of Pythion,
who is praised for having saved the contingents of three
Athenian tribes in a forced march in 446/5 B.C. through the
Boeotian hills. A copy of the Athenian archon list was erected
about 425, probably in the Agora, where the Spartan shields
taken at Pylos were publicly exhibited.[1] Archaistic sculpture
"to emphasize the venerability and permanence of existing
institutions" had begun before 400; and old inscriptions were
cut anew to ensure their preservation.[2]

[1] Peek no. 630 = *IG* I² 1085 = Tod, *GHI*, I, no. 41.
[2] Evelyn B. Harrison, *Archaic and Archaistic Sculpture* (*The Athenian
Agora XI*) (Princeton, 1965), p. 64; contra, Christine M. Havelock, "The
Archaic as Survival versus the Archaistic as a New Style," *American
Journal of Archaeology,* LXIX (1965), pp. 331–40; and also ibid.,

Interestingly enough an appeal to the historical past came to be considered useful for purposes of the present. This was not new—at the battle of Plataea both Tegea and Athens had advanced historical as well as mythical justifications for their respective claims to the post of honor—but it now developed into a convention. The sophist Thrasymachus, for instance, began an oratorical display toward the end of the century, "I could wish, men of Athens, to have belonged to that long-time past when the young were content to remain silent." Equally suggestive of reverence for the past is his further comment that in the clash of parties "the 'ancestral constitution' is a cause of dissension between them, though it is easiest to grasp and is the common property of all citizens." [3]

These are straws in the rising wind, but no more; we may not properly infer from them that by the later fifth century men were growing accustomed to think historically as a natural procedure. The inheritance from earlier days which predisposed the Greeks to look at their world quite otherwise was not so easily set aside, and the audience which listened to historians such as Herodotus or Hellanicus did so with only a small part of its attention.

Those who bought red-figured vases had no interest in acquiring direct portrayals of political leaders or events; as we have noted at several points, even Persians were presented rarely. Coin designers referred cryptically, if at all, to contemporary events by adding a crown of olive leaves or the like; and several famous series of Greek coins, such as the Attic "owls," deliberately preserved archaic types. References to specific events are very uncommon in epitaphs; [4] when poets

LXVIII (1964), pp. 43–58. Copy of the inscription for the Athenian victory over Boeotia and Chalcis in 506: Tod, *GHI*, I, no. 43; a vase by the Pan painter may represent the monument (Harrison, pl. 65a).

[3] Thrasymachus fr. 1. Plataea: Herodotus 9.26–7. Note also the argument of Sosicles from earlier Corinthian history (Herodotus 5.92); and cf. 6.106.2, 7.161.3, 8.142.3. For use of myth in this way, see p. 81.

[4] Coins: See my essay, "The Awakening of the Greek Historical Spirit and Early Greek Coinage," *Numismatic Chronicle* (forthcoming); cf.

gave examples, these still came mainly from mythology and from the epics. In one of his plays, the *Eumenides*, Aeschylus probably had in mind a contemporary reduction in the powers of the Areopagus, and in others Euripides seems to have been speaking to his audience about the horrors of the Peloponnesian War; but, apart from a rare play like the *Persians*, contemporary conditions did not directly appear on the tragic stage. Nor were the comedies of Aristophanes, for all their current jokes, historically minded in any major degree.

From this background stemmed one of the greatest thinkers in Greek civilization, Plato, who had the further misfortune—historically speaking—of drawing particularly on the abstract thought of Parmenides. Insofar as Plato sought to fathom the purpose of human existence, his views have occasionally been called historical; [5] but for history in the sense of a factual recountal of the past he had extraordinarily little concern. If his views really were the touchstone of Greek thought, an assumption often made by modern scholars, then the sweeping characterization of it as "unhistorical," as observed in the Introduction, would be valid.

Actually, however, it is in Plato's era, the fourth century, that history did gain respectability and utility. Several men sought to continue Thucydides' interrupted tale, and historical compositions were ever more common and varied in subject. On this work we need not tarry, for the present study is not a survey of Greek historiography as such. But it is worth noticing how deeply the historical attitude sank its roots into general patterns of Greek thought during the fourth century.

Ch. Picard, *Études thasiennes*, VIII (Paris, 1962), p. 63, for the use of an archaic script and motif on coins of Thasos at the end of the fifth century.

Epitaphs: Peek nos. 73, 305, 888, 915, 916, 1224, 1226, 2043; nos. 13 and 16 also refer respectively to the Eurymedon and Cyprus. See also Tod, *GHI*, I, no. 37 (Selinus *c.*450), 26 (list of Erechtheis dead), 48 (for the dead at Potidaea, which gives only the fact that there they died).

[5] Chatelet, *La Naissance de l'histoire*, pp. 155–7, 229.

Aristotle and his students, in approaching a problem, sought generally to discover its historical development; to this end they drew up chronological lists and assembled histories of constitutions, of philosophy, and of other subjects. As one recent student of Greek tragedy says, "A reasoned view of the origin of a specific literary genre such as tragedy, or even the raising of the question, is inconceivable before the fourth century and the Lyceum. The fifth century may have entertained the question, 'Who was the inventor . . . of tragedy?' . . . but not as a historical problem." [6] For another great figure of the century, Isocrates, the historical past as well as that of myth was a nourishing force and a source of arguments and moral examples to spur present action.[7] His pupil Ephorus, who wrote the first universal history in Greek, deliberately excluded the age of myth because he felt sound historical sources were lacking for this period.[8]

Not all the history which was turned out thenceforth was great history. The growth of conscious rhetorical and ethical theory, the limited appreciation of fact as truth, and the feeble chronological systems of the Hellenic world combined to weaken the historical products of men like Xenophon, Theopompus, and Duris, and after them in the Roman world of Sallust, Livy, and Tacitus. Nevertheless the principles which Herodotus had upheld almost unconsciously and Thucydides had firmly proclaimed remained the standards by which histo-

[6] Else, *Origin and Early Form of Greek Tragedy*, p. 111, n. 14.
[7] Chatelet, *La Naissance de l'histoire*, pp. 349–50, 376, 379–88. In Xenophon, *Memorabilia* 3.5 and *Cyropedia* 8.7.24, "the history of the past . . . is the best source of instruction."

On the use of historical examples in this period: L. Pearson, "Political Allusions in the Attic Orators," *Classical Philology*, XXXVI (1941), pp. 209–29; S. Perlman, "The Historical Example, Its Use and Importance as Political Propaganda in the Attic Orators," *Scripta Hierosolymitana*, VII (1961), pp. 150–66; G. Schmitz-Kahlmann, "Das Beispiel der Geschichte im politischen Denken des Isocrates," *Philologus*, Supplementband XXXI.4 (1939); and the specific examples adduced in my essay, "Why Did the Greeks Defeat the Persians?" *Parola del Passato*, XVII (1962), pp. 321–32.
[8] Ephorus, *FGrH*, no. 70, F 9.

ries were judged; Cicero bluntly proclaimed, "Who does not know that the first duty of history is to say nothing false, and then to dare to say all that is true?" [9]

If we turn and look back at the simple beginnings of Greek civilization, its unhistorical qualities are evident; but there were potentialities which could eventually produce history. For early Greece evolved the concepts of space, time, and man which were assembled in Herodotus' work to produce genuine history. Their stages of incubation, the principal concern of the present work, must be found in the fragments of poetry, philosophy, and art which still survive from the centuries before that great step. Only as a result of this sharpening of thought, the political consolidation of the Greek state system, and man's conscious self-awareness did Greek society reach the stage in the fifth century where a few thinkers—and an audience at least partially interested—thought in those novel terms we call historical.

The history of Herodotus is the oldest extended prose work still surviving from Greek literature, and in it a man accounted historically to himself and his audience how their world came to be. History has been written ever since in Western civilization, even during the ravages of the Northmen in early mediaeval Europe, in order that the deeds of men might not perish; or, to put this drive in deeper light, to provide an answer in human terms to an ever-enduring problem of mankind, What am I and Why?

[9] Cicero, *de oratore* 2.15 (62). On the ideal of truth in Hellenistic and Roman times, see Welles, *Idea of History in the Near East*, pp. 144–5; and the great outburst by Lucian, *The Way to Write True History*.

BIBLIOGRAPHY

DURING RECENT YEARS there has been a remarkable intensification of attention to the archaic phase of Greek civilization, 700–500 B.C. As a result I cannot hope to list here all the pertinent monographs; my aim is rather to suggest works which may lead the interested reader further. More recent books have accordingly been emphasized if they are generally sound (or, occasionally, unsound but provocative) and contain bibliographical guides to earlier studies. Specialized studies cited in chapter notes are not normally repeated.

In *The Origins of Greek Civilization, 1100–650 B.C.* (New York, 1961) I have tried to present a coherent account of the preceding stage of Greek development; this contains extensive references to archaeological and other materials. See also M. I. Finley, *The World of Odysseus* (New York: Meridian Library, 1959).

Archaic culture itself is magisterially surveyed by Hermann Fränkel, *Dichtung und Philosophie des frühen Griechentums* (2d ed.; Munich, 1962), and Werner Jaeger, *Paideia: Die Formung des griechischen Menschen*, I (3d ed.; Berlin, 1954). Bruno Snell, *The Discovery of the Mind* (New York: Harper Torchbook, 1960), is thought-provoking; the same cannot be said for R. B. Onians, *The Origins of European Thought about the Body, the Mind, the Soul, the World, Time and Fate* (2d ed.; Cambridge, 1954), which I cite only because its title suggests more than its text provides. A. R. Burn, *The Lyric Age of Greece* (New York, 1960), is useful for its facts and notes. See also Thorleif Boman, *Hebrew Thought Compared*

152

with Greek (Philadelphia, 1960), and J.-P. Vernant, *Les Origines de la pensée grecque* (Paris, 1962), both of which must be approached with caution.

LITERATURE. Among recent surveys that of Albin Lesky, *A History of Greek Literature* (New York, 1966), is distinguished in judgment and the excellence of its bibliography; I have referred to it often for this reason, to avoid elaboration of footnotes. Relevant particularly to our period are Max Treu, *Von Homer zur Lyrik* (Munich, 1955); and C. M. Bowra, *Greek Lyric Poetry from Alcman to Simonides* (2d ed.; Oxford, 1961), and *Early Greek Elegists* (Cambridge, Mass., 1938). B. A. van Groningen, *La Composition littéraire archaïque grecque* (2d ed.; Groningen, 1960), is of great value though it does not discuss Herodotus himself.

Specialized works of value are Otfrid Becker, *Das Bild des Weges und verwandte Vorstellungen im frühgriechischen Denken, Hermes,* Einzelschrift IV (Berlin, 1937); W. Luther, *"Wahrheit" und "Lüge" im ältesten Griechentum* (Leipzig, 1935); Robert Oehler, *Mythologische Exempla in der älteren griechischen Dichtung* (Aarau, 1925). Tom F. Driver, *The Sense of History in Greek and Shakespearean Drama* (New York, 1960), is weak on the Greek side.

PHILOSOPHY. Within the vast literature on early Greek philosophy I have cited W. K. C. Guthrie, *A History of Greek Philosophy,* I: *The Earlier Presocratics and the Pythagoreans* (Cambridge, 1962); II: *The Presocratic Tradition from Parmenides to Democritus* (Cambridge, 1965), most commonly, for it is the most recent large-scale work (with references to Zeller and other accounts). Useful primarily for their extended discussions are the studies in the Biblioteca di Studi Superiori (Florence); Mario Untersteiner, *Senofane* (1956), and *Parmenide* (1958); M. T. Cardini, *Pitagorici,* 2 vols. (1958–62); Mario Untersteiner (and Antonio Battegazzore for Vol. IV), *Sofisti,* 4 vols. (1949–62). G. S. Kirk and J. E. Raven,

The Presocratic Philosophers (Cambridge, 1960), is more incisive; there is value too in John Burnet, *Early Greek Philosophy* (New York: Meridian Library, 1957).

Specialized studies of utility in the present connection are Felix Heinimann, *Nomos und Physis* (Basel, 1945); Werner Jaeger, *The Theology of the Early Greek Philosophers* (Oxford, 1947); and connected with this latter aspect M. P. Nilsson, *Geschichte der griechischen Religion,* I (2d ed.; Munich, 1955), and E. R. Dodds, *The Greeks and the Irrational* (Boston: Beacon reprint, 1957).

ART. Here too the literature is vast. I owe much to Georg Karo, *Greek Personality and Archaic Sculpture* (Cambridge, Mass., 1948). The recent studies on Greek sculpture by G. M. A. Richter, *Handbook of Greek Art* (London, 1959), *Kouroi* (2d ed.; London, 1960), *Archaic Gravestones of Attica* (London, 1961), and *Portraits of the Greeks* (London, 1965), are well illustrated. For pottery see R. M. Cook, *Greek Painted Pottery* (London, 1960); J. D. Beazley, *Development of Attic Black-figure* (Berkeley, 1951), and *Attic Red-figure Vase-Painters*, 3 vols. (2d ed.; Oxford, 1963), a basic research tool; M. C. Robertson, *Greek Painting* (Geneva, 1959). See also Helmut Schoppa, *Die Darstellung der Perser in der griechischen Kunst bis zum Beginn des Hellenismus* (Coburg, 1933); and Karl Schefold, *Frühgriechische Sagenbilder* (Munich, 1964), and *Griechische Kunst als religiöses Phänomen* (Hamburg, 1959).

T. B. L. Webster, *Greek Art and Literature, 700–530 B.C.* (New York, 1960), and *Greek Art and Literature, 530–400 B.C.* (Oxford, 1939), are interesting comparative studies. For two other arts, see A. W. Lawrence, *Greek Architecture* (Harmondsworth, 1957), and the references in my essay, "The Awakening of the Greek Historical Spirit and Early Greek Coinage," *Numismatic Chronicle* (forthcoming).

POLITICAL DEVELOPMENT. I omit here political histories

of Greece; for the development of political institutions and concepts see Victor Ehrenberg, *The Greek State* (New York: Norton Library, 1964); C. Hignett, *History of the Athenian Constitution to the End of the Fifth Century B.C.* (Oxford, 1952); Victor Martin, *La Vie internationale dans la Grèce des cités* (*VIᵉ-IVᵉ s. av. J.-C.*) (Paris, 1940). P. Lévèque and P. Vidal-Naquet, *Clisthène l'Athénien: essai sur la représentation de l'espace et du temps dans la pensée politique grecque de la fin du VIᵉ siècle à la mort du Platon* (Paris, 1964), is thought-provoking, but the treatment does not quite match the promise of the title. Two classics are Fustel de Coulanges, *The Ancient City* (New York: Anchor reprint, 1956), and A. E. Zimmern, *Greek Commonwealth* (5th ed.; Oxford, 1961). From a different angle see R. E. Wycherley, *How the Greeks Built Cities* (2d ed.; London, 1962).

H. I. Marrou, *History of Education in Antiquity* (New York, 1956), may not fit here entirely but cannot be passed over. Other works on political and social values are suggested in the footnotes to Chapter IV.

IDEAS OF TIME. A fundamental study is Hermann Fränkel, "Die Zeitauffassung in der frühgriechischen Literatur." *Wege und Formen frühgriechischen Denkens* (Munich, 1960), pp. 1–22, though unfortunately he limits his view almost entirely to *chronos;* in this respect Silvio Accame, "La Concezione del tempo nell'età omerica e arcaica," *Rivista di filologia,* n.s. XXXIX (1961), pp. 359–94, goes further. The concept of time has been much debated in modern literature, as the notes to Chapter III will suggest; further introductions may be found in A. D. Momigliano, "Time in Ancient Historiography," *History and Theory,* Beiheft VI (1966), pp. 1–23, and my succeeding essay in the same Beiheft, "Historical and Philosophical Time." Let me, however, single out as particularly relevant B. A. van Groningen, *In the Grip of the Past* (Leiden, 1953), for the breadth of aspects there considered, and Victor Goldschmidt, *Le Système stoïcien et l'idée de temps* (Paris, 1953), for comparative purposes; useful too is P. Vidal-Naquet, "Temps des dieux et temps des hommes," *Revue de l'histoire des religions*, CLVII (1960), pp. 55–80.

For chronology proper see John Forsdyke, *Greece before Homer: Ancient Chronology and Mythology* (New York: Norton Library, 1964); Elias Bickerman, *Chronologie* (2d ed.; Leipzig, 1963).

IDEAS OF SPACE. J. O. Thomson, *History of Ancient Geography* (Cambridge, 1948), is a good account. On ethnography as considered here see recently H. C. Baldry, *The Unity of Mankind in Greek Thought* (Cambridge, 1965); Hans Schwabl et al., *Entretiens Hardt VIII: Grecs et Barbares* (Geneva, 1961); the older work of Julius Jüthner, *Hellenen und Barbaren* (Leipzig, 1923), deserves notice. See also Helen H. Bacon, *Barbarians in Greek Tragedy* (New Haven, 1961).

IDEAS OF HISTORY. I came to François Chatelet, *La Naissance de l'Histoire: la formation de la pensée historienne en Grèce* (Paris, 1962), after the ideas advanced in the preceding pages were already well formulated; while pleased to find that he also emphasizes the need for a historical outlook as a prerequisite to formal history, I mistrust his narrow emphasis on political factors. Mircea Eliade, *Cosmos and History* (New York: Harper Torchbook, 1959), forces one to think as to *why* the Greeks could develop a historical spirit, rather than taking it for granted.

General surveys, such as J. T. Shotwell, *The Story of Ancient History* (New York: Columbia paperback, 1961), or J. B. Bury, *The Ancient Greek Historians* (New York: Dover reprint, 1958), are of limited value for the period covered in this book. More relevant are Lionel Pearson, *Early Ionian Historians* (Oxford, 1939), and *The Local Historians of Attica* (Lancaster, Pa., 1942); and the essays of Felix Jacoby, *Atthis: The Local Chronicles of Ancient Athens* (Oxford, 1949), *Abhandlungen zur griechischen Geschichtschreibung* (Leiden,

1956), and *Griechische Historiker* (Stuttgart, 1956), the latter of which includes his long study of Herodotus from PW. A. W. Gomme, *The Greek Attitude to Poetry and History* (Berkeley, 1959), is level-headed; see also Hermann Peter, *Wahrheit und Kunst: Geschichtsschreibung und Plagiat im klassischen Altertum* (Leipzig, 1911). Essays of value include Karl Reinhardt, "Philosophy and History among the Greeks," *Greece and Rome,* 2d ser. I (1954), pp. 82–90; Wolfgang Schadewaldt, "Die Anfänge der Geschichtsschreibung bei den Griechen," *Die Antike,* X (1934), pp. 144–68; Bruno Snell, "Homer und die Entstehung des geschichtlichen Bewusstseins bei den Griechen," *Varia Variorum* (Münster-Köln, 1952), pp. 2–12; Hermann Strasburger, *Die Wesensbestimmung der Geschichte durch die antike Geschichtsschreibung* (Wiesbaden, 1966), and others of his essays. See also the discussion spurred by Kurt Latte, "Die Anfänge der griechischen Geschichtsschreibung," *Entretiens Hardt IV: Histoire et historiens dans l'antiquité* (Geneva, 1956), pp. 3–37. A general bibliography is given by G. T. Griffiths, *Fifty Years of Classical Scholarship,* ed. Maurice Platnauer (Oxford, 1954), pp. 150–6.

For Herodotus one will find useful *Herodot: Eine Auswahl aus der neueren Forschung* ed. Walter Marg (Munich, 1962). See also J. L. Myres, *Herodotus: Father of History* (Oxford, 1953); Max Pohlenz, *Herodot: Der erste Geschichtschreiber des Abendlandes* (Leipzig, 1937); Aubrey de Selincourt, *The World of Herodotus* (London, 1962); other works of value are included in the notes to Chapter VI. Recently C. Hignett, *Xerxes' Invasion of Greece* (Oxford, 1963), has upheld Herodotus' reliability in general.

INDEX

Acusilaus, 116 n., 144
Aeschylus, 48, 52, 54, 73, 95, 131, 135, 149
Agora, 46, 72, 82, 84, 86
aion, 70
aitia, 7, 103
Alcaeus, 42, 50, 71, 86–8
Alcmaeon, 75, 96, 106, 113
Alcman, 45 n., 87, 105
aletheia: see truth
alphabet, 30–1
Anacreon, 105, 106, 122
Anaximander, 45, 47, 52, 68, 73, 101, 103, 106
annals, 29, 116
Antiochus, 135
Archaic era, 37–41, 58–60, 78–81, 99–100, 117–19
Archilochus, 39, 42, 50, 53, 65, 71, 86, 87, 94
aristocracy, 63, 79, 87–8, 103
Aristogeiton, 84, 122
Aristotle, 9, 20, 55, 59, 75, 77, 110, 150
art: *see* pottery; sculpture
astronomy, 45, 60
Athens, and history, 46, 63, 67, 72, 81–4, 86, 89–90, 94, 96, 132–5
audience, 4, 85–90, 102, 133–5

Bacchylides, 131
barbarians, 49–56, 124, 136–7
biography, 98, 147

Callinus, 66, 71
causation, 91, 94, 103–4, 129–30, 140
change, 8, 58–9, 61–77, 137–9
Charon, 135
chronology, 29, 57–8, 72, 83, 125, 138
chronos, 16, 34, 63 n., 65 n., 67–8, 70, 76–7, 115 n., 124, 131, 137
city-state: see *polis*
Clisthenes, 46, 81, 90, 94
coinage, 43, 82, 148
colonization, 41–3
conservatism, 61–4, 69
cycles, 10, 33, 60, 75, 139

Dark Ages, 8, 21–3, 30, 61
divine will: *see* gods
Egypt, 25–7, 31, 41, 50, 54, 137, 144
ephemeros, 65
Ephorus, 150
epic, influence of on history, 9, 23–5; *see also* Homer
epic cycle, 14, 38
ethnography, 49–56
Euripides, 55, 149

geography, 15, 47–9
gods, 8, 17, 28, 61, 75, 91–7, 104, 109, 129–30, 140
Greek civilization: *see* Dark Ages; Archaic era

Harmodius, 84, 122
Hebrew historiography, 3, 27–9
Hecataeus, 4, 31, 47, 52, 72, 101, 114–15, 143, 144
Hellanicus, 72, 82, 134
Hellas, 31, 53–6, 124
Heraclitus, 28, 64, 101, 104, 110
Herodotus: life and history, 3–7, 9, 25, 29–32, 79, 83, 85–6, 88, 103, 132 ff.; on cause, 7, 104, 140–1; historical spirit, 11, 120; on truth, 19, 111–12, 117, 142–5; on space, 45–6, 48, 56, 136; objectivity, 53–4, 136–7, 145; on time, 58, 72, 73, 77, 126, 137–9; on man, 94–5, 97, 139–41; style, 106, 146
Hesiod, 29, 32–4, 44, 53, 61, 65, 71, 87, 108–9, 127
Hipponax, 105
Hippocrates: see On Airs Waters Places
historia, 6–7, 110, 112–13, 115
history: nature of, 3, 11, 14, 18, 78, 91, 105, 107; Greek limits on 7–11, 18, 21–6, 76, 148–9; see also gods; Herodotus; logographers
Homer, 4, 12–25, 35, 38, 44, 49, 65, 91–2, 107–9
Homeric Hymns, 38, 44, 71, 105
hybris, 97, 130–1

Iliad: see Homer
individualism, 9, 17, 97–8, 147
inscriptions, 50, 82–3, 93, 147
Isocrates, 55, 85, 150

kairos, 70

Lelantine War, 46, 80
logographers, 106, 114–17
logos, 115–16, 143

man, Greek view of, 16–18, 25, 37–8, 91–8, 126–32, 139–41
maps, 47–8, 117, 124
Marathon, 83, 84, 95, 122, 135
medicine, 113–14; see also On Airs Waters Places
Mimnermus, 66, 67, 69, 88
myth, 8–10, 18–25, 72, 123

narrative, 25, 106, 116, 118, 122
Near East: development, 13, 25, 41, 50, 61; historiography, 26–30
nomos, 7, 53, 128, 147

objectivity, 24, 104, 145
Odyssey: see Homer
On Airs Waters Places, 49, 104, 132
On Ancient Medicine, 74, 114, 117, 132

Parmenides, 45, 63–4, 101, 107, 110, 112
Persia, 13, 29–30, 50–1, 133, 137
Persian Wars, 54, 120–1, 128, 135
personality: see individualism; man, Greek view of
Pherecydes of Leros, 134, 144
Pherecydes of Syros, 68, 106
philosophy, 9, 34, 45–6, 59–60, 63–4, 75, 100–4, 108–13
physis, 98, 140, 147
Pindar, 45, 48, 76, 77, 86, 96, 97, 124–31

Plato, 28, 59, 64, 74, 129, 149
poetry: *see names of individual poets*
polis, 7, 54, 78–82, 86–90, 94, 96, 131
political history, 43, 46, 80–2, 128
pottery, 18, 35–6, 39, 48, 51–2, 66, 92–3, 105, 118–19, 121–3, 148
progress, theory of, 73–6
prose, 47, 106
Pythagoras, 88, 96, 101, 112

rationalism, 94, 99–102, 141–2
records, public, 31, 82–3, 116
rhetoric, 111, 146, 150

Sappho, 50, 71, 87, 122
sculpture, 9, 19, 21, 39, 77, 84, 92, 95, 98, 101, 123, 147
Simonides, 65, 69, 101, 123, 135
society, 21, 42–3, 86–90
Solon, 42, 46, 50, 67, 73, 82, 89–90, 94, 99, 103, 108
sophists, 53, 75, 109, 146, 147
Sophocles, 68, 73, 130

space, sense of, 15, 43–9, 58, 124, 131, 136
Sparta, 47, 63, 66, 72, 81, 89, 94

Thales, 45, 93, 101
Themistocles, 83, 84, 145
Theognis, 63, 71, 88, 101, 119, 127–8
Thucydides, 5, 7, 11, 20, 31, 55, 73, 77, 104, 133, 139, 141–4, 146, 150
time, 15–16, 21, 28, 33–4, 57–77, 124–6, 131
tragedy, influence of on history, 132, 141; *see also* Aeschylus
travels, 50–1, 136
treaties, 82
Trojan War: *see* Homer
trophies, 83, 135, 147
truth, 10, 33, 107–15, 117, 127, 142–5, 150–1
Tyrtaeus, 66, 89

Xanthus, 46, 115
Xenophanes, 45, 53, 72, 73, 88, 101, 104, 109, 112, 123
Xenophon, 55, 150

CHESTER G. STARR was born in Centralia, Missouri, in 1914. He holds a B.A. (1934) and an M.A. (1935) in history from the University of Missouri and a Ph.D. (1938) from Cornell University, and from 1938 to 1940 he was a Fellow of the American Academy in Rome. Since 1940 he has taught history at the University of Illinois, where he became a full professor in 1953, was chairman of the Humanities Division from 1953 to 1955, and on occasion has been chairman of the Department of History. During World War II, Mr. Starr spent two years with the Fifth Army in Italy, serving as chief of the Historical Section of the Fifth Army Headquarters. In 1963 the University of Missouri awarded him a Certificate of Merit as a distinguished graduate and he has received two Guggenheim fellowships. His previously published works include *Roman Imperial Navy* (1941, 1960), *Fifth Army History* in nine volumes (1943–6), *Emergence of Rome as Ruler of the Western World* (1950), *Civilization and the Caesars* (1954), *History of the World* in two volumes, with others (1960), *The Origins of Greek Civilization* (1961), and *History of the Ancient World* (1965). He has also published many articles in learned journals in history and classical studies, here and abroad. Mr. Starr makes his home, with his wife and four children, in Urbana, Illinois.

A NOTE ON THE TYPE

THE TEXT of this book is set in Caledonia, a Linotype face designed by W. A. Dwiggins, the man responsible for so much that is good in contemporary book design and typography. Caledonia belongs to the family of printing types called "modern face" by printers—a term used to mark the change in style of type-letters that occurred about 1800. It has all the hard-working feet-on-the-ground qualities of the Scotch Modern face plus the liveliness and grace that is integral in every Dwiggins "product" whether it be a simple catalogue cover or an almost human puppet.

Composed, printed, and bound by
Kingsport Press, Inc., Kingsport, Tennessee.
Typography and binding based on designs
by WARREN CHAPPELL.